D1798470

Artificial Intelligence

Artificial Intelligence: A No Non-sense Handbook for Business Leaders

BY - TYLER DAWSON

Table of Contents

Introduction

What comes to your mind when you hear the word, artificial intelligence (AI)? Perhaps, you think of a science fiction movie from the likes of Orson Scott Card or other famed authors. Maybe you're thinking of Transformers or Wall-E from Disney. The Disneyization of artificial intelligence has made it seem like it's a world of pure fantasy that only exists within the human imagination. However, the reality is that we are not far away from using AI in everyday life. Our use of AI continues to increase with each passing year. As we use Amazon, streaming music devices, and other AI that predicts our choices, we realize that machines and technology are starting to permeate every aspect of our existence. Our mobile devices also come with features that include AI. Because AI is becoming commonplace, it is crucial that we discover ways that we can use it for our own benefit. AI can also be used for the benefit of businesses. That's where this book comes into play.

You may be wondering what exactly artificial intelligence is? This book is going to explain what it is and why it is important. This book will be a helpful guide used to instruct you on how you can use the information about artificial intelligence in your business and to increase your profitability and benefits. This book will contain vital information, which can help you apply knowledge about AI to your business practices.

Most people, who want to learn about new things, will find that one or two books are not entertaining enough for them, so they give up halfway because the books are full of fluff or information that is not useful or simply boring. This book is not going to be like that. Prepare to be amazed by all that you can discover about AI.

This book will contain helpful and concise chapters on artificial intelligence topics, which can be applied to the workplace. Each chapter includes a basic organization with examples and a case study, which will help illustrate the points explained. The chapters draw upon real-life experiences and sources that can help you to grow your business. We hope that you will enjoy all the discoveries that you find in this book.

This book has 20 chapters. In this first chapter, we will look at the difference between AI and AGI, along with a case study. In the second chapter, we will talk about modern applications of AI with a case study. The third chapter will describe the machine intelligence continuum on which we will chart the development of AI technology from its most primitive origins to its most advanced functions. Chapter 4 discusses the promises and challenges of AI technology, including what a business has to gain from AI technology. In Chapter 5, we discuss safe and ethical AI and how your organization can promote the safe use of AI technology. Chapter 6 is about how you can prepare your workforce for AI in the training and development of your workforce. Chapter 7 talks about how to recruit top technical talent to help you prepare the use of AI in your business. Once you have a strong technical team, then you can start implementing the technology in your business. Chapter 8 describes the implementation process. Chapter 9 will talk about how to collect and prepare data that is useful for the analysis and monitoring of your customer's information and other factors. After that, Chapter 10 discusses building machine learning models, which facilitate the development of successful AI models for your company.

As soon as you have the model ready, then you can experiment and iterate it in Chapter 11. This chapter also highlights two important case studies in experimentation that can be used in your company. With all these opportunities, there will also be obstacles to be confronted, as you will find out in Chapter 12. Yet, there are also solutions to manage all these difficulties. In Chapter 13, you will find out more about how AI can be a solution to the problems behind administrative work, which can be grueling and tiresome for human beings, but very efficient and fast for robots. With increased investment in AI technology, bots can help with many transactions. Chapter 14 talks about how robots can be used in the recruitment process and the implications for human resources in the future. In the next chapter, you will find out more about business intelligence and analytics, including the different kinds of strategies used by companies to forecast customer data. In Chapter 16, we dive into software development and how AI can help with designing software that will be efficient and creative. Chapter 17 talks about marketing strategies, which are driven by customer data. Chapter 18 describes sales techniques, which take advantage of AI, and making forecasts and scoring leads. Chapter 19 describes the future of customer service, which will be driven by AI. Finally, the last chapter talks about the Ethics of Enterprise AI.

Are you a manager, owner of your own company, or an associate of an organization? This book is for you. You can learn about all the things that will help your business to flourish amid an economy that is increasingly influenced by AI technology. We know that you will benefit from using this book to discover all that you want to know about the basics of AI and its practical applications. We provide everything that business leaders need to know about artificial intelligence and lead you to the road of discovery. Let's go on this road together, to the future, and beyond!

Chapter : 1
AI vs. AGI

"Artificial intelligence will reach human levels by around 2029. Follow that out further to, say, 2045, and we will have multiplied the intelligence, the human biological machine intelligence of our civilization a billion-fold."

– Ray Kurzweil (Brown, 2019)

We've all seen the movies where the robots take over the planet, with their mechanical parts making headlines. This is what Hollywood likes to talk about. While these films lead us into an alternate reality for a few hours, we still have the thought in the back of our heads, which indicates that this could happen to us in the future. Robots and AI are not a new concept (Davey, n.d.). The father of AI, Alan Turing, talked about it in the 1950s. He developed the Turing Test, which talks about what it means to be a machine and a human being.

Today, AI has evolved into a lot of things with the advancements in technology. However, it is still a new field of research, which continues to evolve, and scientists are continually coming up with ways that they can best use the innovations to create the films. But because the field is new, we cannot simply think that machines are going to take over any time soon (Davey, n.d.).

Terms like AI and AGI have been continually redefined over time so that we can better understand their differences.

What is Artificial Intelligence (AI)?

In our Hollywoodization of the term AI, we might think of C-3PO from Star Wars or a robot from the movie, Wall-E. But it is important for you to remove these images from your mind because the way Hollywood makes you think about these mechanical characters is not reflective of reality.

AI simply refers to a machine, which can replicate human cognition, including abilities like solving problems and learning. But here's the thing: human programming is always involved in these creations. So, the human has to be the first mover in the entire process, the prime mover as Aristotle would call it.

Take playing chess, for example. A human has to make the moves with the pegs, but the computer can make a move on a virtual chessboard by using data and command functions (Davey, n.d.). You can't analyze medical data, because that information must be programmed into the computer.

AI allows for an automated way to do a human task. However, instead of using people's power to go through a lot of data, it allows the machine to complete the action in less time. Conversely, AI functions must be programmed by a human being first.

Now, business owners want to include AI in their processes, and 72% of business leaders think that AI will help their future business to succeed (Davey, n.d.).

What is Artificial General Intelligence (AGI)?

Although AI is pre-programmed to carry out a human task, AGI expects the machine to carry out action just as well as a human and to be just as intelligent as a human (Davey, n.d.).

This is the kind of AI that we see in Hollywood. AGI machines theoretically can do everything that a human can do intellectually at the same rate of speed or even better.

Apple co-founder, Steve Wozniak, created a task known as the Coffee Test, which determines if a machine is AGI or not. In the test, the robot goes into a house and makes a cup of coffee but has no specific programming instructions to do so. It just does the task freely. If a machine could carry out this function, including assembling all the parts of a cup of coffee, including the filter, brewing, etc., then it would be a good example of AGI. An AI machine could tell you how much coffee you would need to use based on previously inputted data from a human being; however, it wouldn't be able to sort through the entire process of making a cup of coffee. You can teach a non-programmed machine to do almost anything without any help, which can be done without any programming whatsoever.

By 2030, we might have AGI machines who will be servers, shop attendants, and bag carriers, and who might also be able to replace human counterparts (Davey, n.d.) In as little as ten years from now, we might have robots taking over the world because every day we're getting a little closer to that reality.

Until that time, however, the concept of AI and AGI continues to take place.

Case Study

Henry and Eric were at a conference about AI last week. They wanted to know the differences between AI and AGI, so they went to different sessions, which highlighted for them what distinctions they could draw. Henry talked to Kelly James, who was the speaker of the conference. Kelly said, "You know, AI is something that is always changing. We don't look at AI the same way we used to in the past. Don't believe what Wall-E and other movies are telling you about robots. Robots can be beneficial to our humanity and will not take over and kill everyone in the world. Actually, they are for the good of humanity and for the objectives of the human race, so you shouldn't fear them. What you should know about AI and AGI is that one of them is simulating the capacities of human thought and development, but they are both still robots. There will never be a time in which robots will simply operate without the help and programming skills of people. Humans will always have their hand in the job, so you shouldn't think for one second that the world is going to turn into a dystopia as you see in science fiction movies. It really is out there and does not correspond with reality."

We have misconceptions about AI and what it means; however, we must think about how AI is going to build up humanity and not tear it down. These days, many people are hesitant to recommend the use of robots, because of prejudice and bias against it. However, there are many benefits that we should examine.

Chapter 2: Modern Applications of AI

"What is vital is to make anything about AI explainable, fair, secure, and with lineage, meaning that anyone could see very simply see how any application of AI developed and why."

– Ginni Rometty (Brown, 2019)

While not a new concept, AI permeates everything that we do in our lives. You may wonder how AI is affecting your life right now. Automation and regulation are always happening while we're on the Internet and using our GPS. These tech gadgets have been pre-programmed by human beings for the purpose of improving our everyday lives. And they help us do a variety of different things. You may be wondering: what are these items? How does AI apply to my life? Let's look at some key examples of AI, which are in your neck of the woods.

1. Siri

Everyone knows Apple's personal assistant, which is a voice-activated system that we see every day (Adams, 2017). Siri uses data from the Internet to find information, gives us directions to different places, adds things to our to-do list and events to our calendar, helps send instant messages, among other things. Siri uses machine-learning technology to predict and understand our various choices and requests. With all Apple users, we can safely say that Siri is the AI tool that is used regularly by millions of people throughout the world. Later, you will see how relevant it is to update your knowledge of AI (Adams, 2017).

2. Alexa

Alexa is a modern invention, which was first introduced by Amazon (Adams, 2017). It is used to decipher speech from anywhere in a room. With its ultra-smart voice activation system, it allows you to search the web, make appointments, set alarms, and many other requests. With millions of Amazon users in the US, it is clear that your modern application of AI is constantly at your finger-tips. Additionally, Amazon will help predict which products you will buy and will give you recommendations on what you can buy. This can be a great marketing technique.

3. Tesla

Do you remember the famous invention wizard, Tesla? Perhaps you have seen the 2005 epic film, The Prestige, and can remember how the magic came about. Tesla is also one of the greatest cars on the planet due to its automated features and technological accolades. The cars are smart and have self-driving capacities. Additionally, they are being updated on a regular basis.

4. Cogito

As a powerful example of behavioral adaptation, Cogito improves emotional intelligence in customer service (Adams, 2017). It involves the fusion of machine learning and behavioral science and allows for improvement in customer-merchant interactions. It provides support for customer service professionals, who have to interact with countless people every day.

5. Boxever

This item uses machine learning to improve the customer experience in the travel industry. This product continues to dominate the industry, and it allows customers to contact and interact with their customers during their travels.

6. John Paul Concierge Services

This is a famous concierge service provider, which is used by various companies, including Visa, Orange, and Air France (Adams, 2017).

7. Amazon Prime and the Marketplace

Amazon uses AI to make millions of transactions every day, which has also generated a large revenue source. Every year, the tool improves and benefits the customers in a variety of great ways. The algorithms being used by the company enables the company to have more development in technology. There is a rumor that the AI from Amazon has the ability to ship out products before they are even ordered. Although this aspect of Amazon has not yet been materialized, as it is still in the works, someday, the company will be able to anticipate buyers' requests even before they make them. That is, however, a slightly foreboding notion, as well.

8. Netflix

We all enjoy watching Netflix when we get home from the office or school. Netflix allows us to enjoy different aspects of films, which in turn also allows us to have fun. Netflix realizes how much we love our movies and analyzes customer reactions to films watched and suggests films for people, which are based on previous choices made (Adams, 2017). Most of the movies highlighted are very popular movies, while no-name or independent movies typically are not mentioned.

9. Pandora and Spotify

Music streaming services are becoming more sophisticated these days. Gone are the days when you would buy a CD. All of our music is online or can be put onto our mobile devices. Online streaming platforms, such as Pandora and Spotify, use AI to recommend songs to the listeners, which helps them to dig deeper into the various music choices that they have (Adams, 2017). It's very helpful to have music choices already given to you, so you can explore and discover new music that you have never heard before, but really enjoy.

Case Study

Sam didn't realize how much he was using AI until his computer science professor pointed it out to him. He wasn't really interested in computer science and was taking an introduction course, but the professor gave him an interesting take on it. Sam said, "I don't understand the point of this. Why do we need to know about AI? Aren't robots too outlandish to be even considered part of our lives? Come on, I've seen Star Wars and Star Trek a hundred times. I know that it is all is too far from reality." Professor Wilkes responded, "You know, Sam. Think about it. How much do you use your phone?" "A lot," said Sam. The professor said, "Do you know that your phone is filled with AI-powered functions? I'm sure that you use Google Maps or GPS systems to get somewhere. Right?" "Yes, that's right. I do use Google Maps almost everywhere now," said Sam. The professor continued, "Well, Sam, you've got to understand that AI is everywhere and that it is continuing to influence your life, whether you like it or not. You just have to see how useful and amazing it is, because it is changing our lives forever." Professor Wilkes pointed out one potential use of AI technology in individual lives. It is important to bear in mind that there are countless ways that AI can be applied to our various situations.

Conclusion

It is evident that AI has the ability to impact our lives in the various technology sources that we use every day. We are constantly influenced by AI, whether that is listening to music on the subway through Apple Music on our mobile devices or doing some online shopping on Amazon. Although it may seem mythical or dystopian, it is important to dispel the myths behind it. AI is real-world based, and it is grounded in reality. And it is going to help the human race to get better at what it does best, and in creativity and innovation.

Chapter : 3
Machine Intelligence Continuum

In this chapter, we will talk about the machine intelligence continuum, which helps to organize the ideas behind AI.

To simplify things for people, in order to better understand the applications of AI, a machine intelligence continuum was designed. Machine Intelligence Continuum (MIC) is the continuum from simple and scripted automation in AI technology to the use of superhuman abilities (Yao, 2017). In other words, it highlights how robots can do the many fancy things that they can do from being programmed to being autonomous objects.

Let's look at the continuum of AI objects, which begins with items that are pre-programmed to work.

Systems that Act

A system that acts is one that responds automatically to a given stimulus based on previous programming. A smoke detector is an example. It contains a sensor monitoring smoke levels and once an environment has reached a certain level, it automatically goes off. Another example is cruise control when you're driving a car. When you drive your car on a highway at 80 mph, the cruise control will look at your car's speed and will use the car's motor and maintain a constant speed (Yao, 2017). However, note that this is not the case of a self-driving car. Instead, it is an object that can move based on human commands.

Systems that Predict

With these systems, the AI device will analyze the data and make predictions that are based on that data. "A prediction" is not necessarily for an eventual happening, but the mind mapping of known and unknown information. A man named Andrew Pole did an experiment where he was asked to identify twenty-five different random items, including lotion and vitamin supplements, which can be used to predict if a person will become pregnant, as well as the stages of the pregnancy (Yao, 2017).

Systems that predict will use automated technology. It will produce advertisements that are well-timed, which trigger consumption from pregnant shoppers. The wrong data, however, can cause these predictions to come up with the wrong solutions, which will lead to skewed results (Yao, 2017).

One example of how this misconception came about was during the 2016 US Election, in which data integrity and methodological mistakes caused a big problem in terms of accuracy leading to erroneous conclusions.

Systems that Learn

The next type of AI system is one that learns. With this type of system, the AI device has the capacity to perform tasks when not programmed to do so. It also can make predictions like statistical systems do and function at human and better-than-human levels (Yao, 2017). This system also carries out automated tasks, such as acquiring the data, which then makes predictions about the world. It requires a higher level of judgment and action to produce a result.

This system is more complex and can include self-driving cars and industrial robotics. These machines must be able to handle entire tasks autonomously. For example, an automated vehicle must turn the video and sensor feed into correct predictions of the surrounding environments. It would be present while performing online learning and requires real-life data so that the device can apply machine learning techniques and bring about excellent results.

Systems that Create

Although we are the only ones who are creative as human beings, computers have been used to make generative designs for decades. Computational creativity has the capacity to create original music, imagery, graphic designs, writing, among many other things (Yao, 2017). We see this form of AI used in Hollywood for music that is generated by computers, which makes it a lot easier to compose original music and soundtracks.

Systems that Relate

Daniel Goleman is a psychologist who championed the cause for emotional intelligence. In his 1995 book of the same title, Goleman wrote about how much of what we are taught in school emphasizes our IQ and how we can become more intelligent. However, he thought that EQ is actually more important than IQ. What makes a person more successful is not how smart they are, but how emotionally aware, perceptive, and controlled a person is and is able to relate to others around them. With this idea, computer engineers also include this concept as an important one for machines. These days, machines must also be able to identify with the emotions of human beings, as we begin to increase our usage of AI in society. With our continued use of AI in Amazon Echo's Alexa and Apple's Siri, the need for machines to understand human emotions has become more vital.

What machines need to do is understand how to analyze a person's emotional state using sentiment analysis (Yao, 2017). This feature will quantify a person's emotional state from their text, voice, facial expressions, and body language. If a device can detect a person's emotional state, then this will help the computer to respond in an empathetic way, just as humans know how to do.

Emotional intelligence and awareness can help businesses as they conduct their sales and marketing as well as enhance communication. Additionally, it can help improve the effectiveness of brand content selling through monitoring and analyzing consumer reactions to different sets of data.

Systems that Master

Recognizing a tiger is something a child can do from a young age. He or she may see a tiger one time and then can instantly recognize it thereafter as a tiger (Yao, 2017). However, a machine must go through and process countless images of tigers in order to recognize them and sort them. Humans are already systems that can master, because of all the visual and spatial data that we collect every day, which enables us to recognize millions of things in our minds. However, this type of technology is still to be developed for different robots in the future.

Systems that Evolve

The final systems that are the way of the future include systems that evolve. This is the last frontier of AI in which the machines will be able to transform their own architecture effectively. As human beings, we change and develop through genetic mutations across generations rather than re-architecting our own biological infrastructure. But as machines develop themselves, they can reshape their own construction to change with the times (Yao, 2017). It is a far-fetched field, but also may not be too far in the future.

Case Study

Jemima was working in her lab on a project for emotional intelligence. She thought to herself, "I know I'm so fascinated with machine technology that I want to see new AI come about. However, I really want to have devices that understand human emotions and can respond well to what we feel every day. For example, if I am feeling sad and I had a horrible day at school, I want Siri to tell me something that will instantly lift my spirits up." Furthermore, Jemima thought that emotional intelligence could be a helpful way to spruce up devices that need better features. By adding bits of technology to empathize with the user, she was able to conclude that the way of the future is a device that will understand the depths of human emotion. This would help humans to feel better and develop positive psychology that keeps people motivated to be their best selves in society.

Now researchers have developed new AI that can identify with people's feelings and understand how to respond to situations where people are upset or sad about something. Before, people disregarded emotions when discussing machines. But now, empathy is the word of the day when it comes to talking about machine learning. While a machine cannot mimic when a person gets upset, they can understand that a human feels that way and therefore will respond accordingly. It's a powerful thing.

Conclusion

From the machine intelligence continuum, we can conclude that there is a process by which AI structures are progressing from controlled and programmed to autonomous and automated functions. While we tend to think of the Hollywoodish depictions of AI, much of what we use it for is still quite controlled by human functions and commands. Therefore, we are still on the beginning scales of development with AI. We're not that close to developing AI systems that master and evolve. However, we do have AI systems, which are able to predict and monitor data that is acquired. AI can make our lives easier and more efficient. Through using the continuum, we are able to see where on the spectrum we still have to develop before we create devices with superhuman capacities. That day will be an amazing one, for sure.

Chapter : 4
The Promises and Challenges of Artificial Intelligence

"Much has been written about AI's potential to reflect both the best and the worst of humanity. For example, we have seen AI providing conversation and comfort to the lonely; we have also seen AI engaging in racial discrimination. Yet the biggest harm that AI is likely to do to individuals in the short term is job displacement, as the amount of work we can automate with AI is vastly larger than before. As leaders, it is incumbent on all of us to make sure we are building a world in which every individual has an opportunity to thrive."

– Andrew Ng (Brown, 2019)

AI's time may have come to the forefront of science, but a lot of things still must be done. Despite over six decades of development, AI has failed to live up to the hype that surrounded it. Decades have been spent trying to define human intelligence, but the progress has failed to deliver based on the earlier excitement. However, since the 1990s, technological progress has caught up. Machine-learning algorithms have continued to improve through the development of deep machine learning techniques (Manyika and Bughin, 2018).

Now, we can design machines that are able to train more complex models of intelligence. We can use silicon-level innovation with graphic processing of details and store large amounts of data in the cloud.

Currently, massive amounts of data are being generated, and through new developments, we now can train AI algorithms. We have developed system-level innovations, automated vehicles that can function on their own, and satellite technology, which can be used anywhere on the planet.

Most of the progress we have seen has been in the form of narrow AI in natural language processing (NLP). With the advancement of deep learning, we have been able to implement machine learning, which includes constructing artificial neural networks, which are developed to resemble the way that neurons interact in the brain (Manyika and Bughin, 2018). Looking at the human brain, there are deep layers of interconnected neurons, which are responsible for deep learning. Further research is needed to go deeper with this topic and help machines to undergo the same amount of learning.

If we look at the new developments of AI, we should also look at how it is going to help businesses.

Promises for Business

AI will be a transformative vehicle that will completely re-design the structure of businesses. Different kinds of learning will be incorporated, including supervised learning, unsupervised learning, and reinforcement learning. The most practical kind that will be employed will be supervised learning. Within that form, machines will learn how to create a relationship with the given sources of data to recognize images and even transcribe the human voice.

On the other hand, there is unsupervised learning, by which the machine will detect clusters or patterns within a set of data. A machine will be able to decode images of buildings and understand architectural styles, as well.

AI still has a lot of practical challenges, but there are new techniques that are emerging to address them. With machine learning, it is crucial to label training data necessary for supervised learning.

We need to develop deep learning techniques, which will allow the AI to learn well, especially through generalized learning, as well. AI devices continue to struggle with carrying their experiences from one situation to the other. Therefore, we need to develop transfer learning, which allows the AI to transfer a set of skills or experiences from a specific task to learning another activity or skill, which is similar to the one implied (Manyika and Bughin, 2018).

Benefits from AI in Business

Adopting AI will prove to be a tremendous benefit to your organization. AI can increase business performance. For example, it can analyze data from audio and images that can help detect anomalies in assembly lines or aircraft machines (Manyika and Bughin, 2018).

AI can optimize the daily routing of delivery traffic, improve fuel efficiency, and reduce delivery times (Manyika and Bughin, 2018). It can be a tool that is used in call centers for customer service management. With improved speech recognition technology, AI is helping people to manage large customer calls and better delegate tasks. Additionally, it helps us to indicate what kinds of products and services people are willing to invest in, which allows marketing strategies to come into play.

Such practical AI use cases allow all sectors of the economy to benefit from AI. It will help to grow multiple business functions.

Challenge #1: Uneven Adoption of the Technology

One of the challenges of AI in business is that not every business is on board with it. Many businesses are taking it on slowly or not at all. According to the McKinsey study, 50% of businesses have one AI device that is used to help with the business in some way. 30% of businesses are piloting and experimenting with it. Finally, only 21% are using AI in several parts of the business, which is usually in the STEM sector (Manyika and Bughin, 2018).

The challenge for the adoption of AI technology continues. Developing an AI strategy will provide potential benefits for a company. However, finding the right talent for it with appropriate skill sets can be difficult.

Additionally, to develop a neural network that resembles the human brain is an art that requires a lot of expertise and experience. The demand for these skills can supply the needs of the business. However, fewer than 10,000 people can actually handle the problems of AI, and the competition for these positions and skills is very high (Manyika and Bughin, 2018). With low supply, these jobs are meant only for people with highly technical skills.

Benefits for the Economy

AI has the potential to benefit the global economy. Amid rising inflation and declining birth rates, productivity growth continues to be an important factor in today's economy. Productivity growth has continued to level off in developed economies, with an average of 0.5% in 2010 from 2.4% a decade ago (Manyika and Bughin, 2018).

AI could have an economic impact through different means. It could be used for labor substitution, augmentation, and contribution to labor productivity. As it substitutes human labor, it will enable workers to carry out more productive and higher-value work, which will increase the demand and training of workers who can use AI technologies.

In addition, AI could take on a role in boosting human innovation and creativity, which will encourage companies to bring their products to the top of the line. With everyone wanting to work their way to the top economically, more revenue will be generated. And this could result in raising the world GDP by as much as 13 trillion USD by 2030, which would be around a 1.2% increase in GDP (Manyika and Bughin, 2018).

Challenge #2: Readiness of Each Country Varies

On the other hand, the readiness of each country that can use AI is different. Currently, only China and the United States have invested most heavily in AI-research related activities. Next in line are Germany, Japan, and the U.K., which are advancing in their use of AI technology. Finally, there are technologically-minded countries in Europe and Asia, including Belgium, Singapore, South Korea, and Sweden, which are contributing to more research in this field (Manyika and Bughin, 2018).

Aside from these key players, Brazil, India, Italy, and Malaysia operate from a weaker starting position but are increasing their output with more graduates in the STEM areas to contribute more meaningfully to AI.

Challenge #3: AI and Automation

With AI and automation becoming more common, there are major disruptions at work to be expected. Only about half of work-related activities can be automated. Physical activities requiring calculation or data collection are automatable. On the other hand, managing others, providing expertise, and interfacing stakeholders remain deeply tied to human relationships and labor. By some estimates, 30% of all activities in 60% of all occupations can be automated (Manyika and Bughin, 2018). However, only 5% of occupations can be entirely automatable. Therefore, more occupations will be automated partially rather than at 100%.

The Effects on Work

The effects on work are significant in that AI will be able to phase out jobs in the workforce, bring in new jobs, and change the face of some jobs. Jobs in highly developed countries, such as France, Japan, and the United States could be more impacted by automation than jobs in countries like India.

The McKinsey Research Institute estimates that between 2016 to 2030, 15% of the global workplace will be replaced, which is about 400 million workers. To make up for that, 555 million to 890 million jobs could be added (21 to 33% increase) (Manyika and Bughin, 2018). With more people aging and the birth rate declining, there could be a surplus in the number of jobs taken and more work will be available than workers who can fill the vacancies.

Because of automation and other key parts of AI, machines will complement human labor in the workplace. On the other hand, millions of workers with menial skills will need to switch jobs to other tasks that require more technical or intellectual skills that can only be performed by a human being. This includes managers, teachers, tech, and other professionals, gardeners, plumbers, and nursing aids. These occupations are expected to grow in the coming decades (Manyika and Bughin, 2018).

Benefits to Society and Challenges

What AI can bring to society is an ability to overcome the world's challenges. It can provide an emphasis on health and nutrition, equality, and inclusion. However, it is not immune to the possibility of misuse and unintended consequences. Using automation to drive human vehicles could help save thousands of lives every year by reducing accidents. Having a self-driving vehicle could be immensely helpful for our roads, which continually sees accidents that hurt and kill many people every year. In addition, the use of AI will reduce the need for human labor in unsafe environments, including offshore oil rigs and coal mines. These areas are not safe places for humans, and getting rid of human labor in these locations could be helpful in promoting good working conditions. We could also see the deployment of AI in disaster areas after hurricanes, floods, and earthquakes, which will reduce the need to put humans in difficult places that can endanger their lives (Manyika and Bughin, 2018).

Challenge #4: Data Privacy

Another challenge that we see with the implementation of AI is the issue of data privacy and misuse of AI. Many people deal with this problem every day, which includes things like identity theft, the use of passwords online, and stolen credit cards. It is important that we find ways to secure our data because that will enable us to do all things effectively. We want to promote safety and security amid an environment that is filled with thieves and hackers, who want to steal our precious information and use it for their own gain and benefit (Manyika and Bughin, 2018).

Ways to Improve AI to Address these Challenges

There are different ways that we can address these challenges, including labeling the data to help the systems, as they process our information. We should also develop strategies for acquiring data and implementing systems to check and protect the data that we collect. Next, we should explain what the AI machines do to others and provide education and training to individuals in technical matters, which will increase people's perception and awareness of AI issues. Also, we should learn different things and bring them to a domain, whether that is in our workplace or some other place. Then, we can learn how to include AI in our everyday lives and feel like we are growing and improving as a result.

Case Study

Amy and Michael were talking about how AI was going to take over the world and cause a great decline in jobs, which was concerning, considering they were preparing to graduate from college and were trying to decide on a field that they wanted to enter. Here's their conversation.

Amy: Michael, you know that AI is about to take over the world. We're going to lose almost 400 million jobs, according to the McKinsey study. That's massive. I don't see how in the world AI is going to help benefit our lives. Do you know how it's going to do that?

Michael: Well, Amy, if you took a closer look at the remainder of the document, you will find that actually, AI is going to double the number of jobs we already have. Although we're going to see a decline in some non-technical jobs, there will still be an increase in technical and educational fields, which require human labor.

Amy: I know we're both computer education majors, so there is no chance of being phased out. But how do you feel that some people's jobs will be either eliminated or require changes?

Michael: I think it means that people need to become adaptable. Today's world is filled with people who are stagnating and staying in one job for decades, while only pulling in cash. People need to feel challenged and do work that is memorable and meaningful, not just any work. And I think that phasing out some jobs and giving them to robots will do just that.

Amy: Are you sure? Some people are getting older and can no longer train themselves to get a new job after decades of experience. It is a lot harder to get them on board with using AI and other features. Do you think we still need to make them use AI-powered devices?

Michael: Either they can choose to use it or retire. I think that the workforce needs to meet today's pressing demands because technology is going off the charts. More and more people need technology to do day-to-day tasks. That fact is not going to change anytime soon. Therefore, it is crucial that people get on board as soon as possible.

Amy: I see. Thanks, Michael, for talking. I'm so glad that doctors, lawyers, and teachers can be assured of their job security in years to come.

Michael: Indeed. These intellectual fields will never disappear as they require the depth of insight and understanding not required of other fields. They are non-technical but require high-level capacities, which will not ever be mimicked by any kind of machine or device. Therefore, we can enjoy the reassurance that our jobs are protected and will always be valued.

Amy: Thank you, Michael.

Michael: My pleasure.

Conclusion

To sum it up, it is vital that we see that there are numerous challenges and benefits to using AI in our society. AI continues to develop and grow, although it still has not reached a wide-spread usage across the board. Many fields will see AI as complementary to human labor, but not totally replacing it. Because many of the jobs and work-related tasks require human hands, the phasing out of jobs is less likely to happen in the future. However, AI continues to be a marker in replacing the work that is menial and for unskilled workers, which will inevitably push such workers out of the workplace.

On the other hand, it will bring them into a new job, which will require more substantial training. The benefits of using AI will include an increased GDP across the world, new jobs created with highly-skilled tasks, as well as improvement in human labor. These benefits are significant. However, we also must weigh the pros with the cons and see how we can develop new strategies that use AI but do not replace the importance of human labor, which will always be more necessary.

Chapter : 5
Safe and Ethical AI

"Why give a robot an order to obey orders — why aren't the original orders enough? Why command a robot not to do harm — wouldn't it be easier never to command it to do harm in the first place? Does the universe contain a mysterious force pulling entities toward malevolence, so that a positronic brain must be programmed to withstand it? Do intelligent beings inevitably develop an attitude problem? (…) Now that computers really have become smarter and more powerful, the anxiety has waned. Today's ubiquitous, networked computers have an unprecedented ability to make mischief should they ever go to the bad. But the only mayhem comes from unpredictable chaos or from human malice in the form of viruses. We no longer worry about electronic serial killers or subversive silicon cabals because we are beginning to appreciate that malevolence — like vision, motor coordination, and common sense — does not come free with computation but has to be programmed in. (…) Aggression, like every other part of human behavior we take for granted, is a challenging engineering problem!"

– Steven Pinker, How the Mind Works (Artificial Intelligence, Good Reads)

AI has the capacity to bring us to a place that is unpredictable and dangerous, which could be a disaster for everyone involved. How can we ensure that these AI systems remain safe and beneficial to humans? Rosie Campbell, Assistant Director of the Center for Human-Compatible AI (CHAI) at the University of California Berkeley, shares her own thoughts for how we can do this (Manyika and Bughin, 2018).

Campbell says that CHAI's mission is to reorient the field of AI so that it can be beneficial to human systems (Manyika and Bughin, 2018). Human ethics and compatibility need to be built into the definition of AI. Therefore, AI needs to have the purpose of helping human beings. If it does not do this, then it cannot achieve its original goals.

The main problem that CHAI wants to solve is the concept of AI alignment. It is important to note that AI does what we tell them to do and not what we mean to say. Systems should be competent in doing what we tell them to do. Furthermore, we need to have more coordinated efforts and cooperation in helping make progress in this area (Manyika and Bughin, 2018).

Backlash Against Social Media and Manipulation

Functionally, we're seeing how certain problems with AI are affecting social media, for example. There is a lot of backlash against social media, which are developed systems that were designed for engaging people in conversation based on the number of clicks and time spent online. As AI systems discovered that people were producing outrageous content, which was gathering ratings and more clicks, people started to receive more of this content. Moreover, this led people to become more outraged at the system, but it also meant that people were more likely to click on extreme content (Manyika and Bughin, 2018).

Social media systems have become more manipulative, which makes it more likely for us to click on content (Manyika and Bughin, 2018). With the systematic and sophisticated data measurement, these AI devices can predict how we will interact with the content that we view online. They can also measure incentives because our human minds measure what rewards we can gain from interacting online. On the other hand, this does not reflect our personal values and preferences.

How Can CHAI deal with the problem of misaligned AI?

According to Campbell, CHAI plans to build a community of researchers, who can organize different events and host interns. This team will provide a public sphere for AI research and dissemination.

How has CHAI made progress to advancing beneficial AI?

Through Cooperative Inverse Reinforcement Learning, people are gaining more insights into how to use AI. We are learning how we can achieve "corrigibility" in AI systems so that we can correct something when it goes wrong and turn off the machine. This is known as the Off-Switch Game. However, as machines become more advanced, they will become more attuned to the problems of this method and will want to disable the off-switch, which can prevent a person from turning it off. In addition, this method of learning can operate through shared rewards, which helps machines and humans to benefit from the advancements made (Manyika and Bughin, 2018).

Principles for Creating Safer AI

Stuart Russell also developed some insights that are important for how we can improve the safety of AI and integrate them into our public sphere. In a TED talk from 2017, he highlights the ways that AI is growing and developing, but also the challenges that accompany these changes (TED, 2017).

The real world has grown to be more complicated, and, as a result, we have problems with decision-making. With developments in technology still happening, reading, a skill that is fundamental to the human race is not yet happening in machines (TED, 2017). When machines are able to read, they will read everything that the human race has ever written. Furthermore, they will be able to look further ahead than any human could and have access to information that will enable humans to make better decisions. However, is this a good thing?

Our whole civilization is based on our intelligence. If we have more access to intelligence, then we can do anything. A lot of people think that AI might be the end-all for the entire human species. This idea has been around for a while. We continue to struggle with a strange feeling in our stomach that we could make a machine more intelligent than a human. Yet, AI can provide a lot of benefits that are worth considering (TED, 2017).

The purpose we put into machines is the purpose that we want to align with our human values. But the thing is, we may have an objective that doesn't align with our goals. As we look into AI, we have to understand the machines' objectives as fitting with our own aligned objectives (TED, 2017).

A robot's only objective is to maximize the achievement of human values and goals, which is aligned with human preferences. Robots have no interest to protect their own existence. Instead, they must pursue what it is that the human has designed them to do with human values in mind, which the robot is initially uncertain about what these values are. Through observing human choices and behavior, it develops an idea of what a human wants in his or her life. Robots exist for a purely altruistic purpose and must respect the preferences of all humans. However, they do not copy human behavior, which can be nasty and unkind (TED, 2017).

As an AI researcher, Russell talks about how there are researchers who are working on how to align the robot's objectives with human objectives, based on the various preferences of different people. In the future, we will be able to have a conversation with an AI personal assistant, such as Siri, but on a whole new level, which reflects our values. No longer will we rely on an AI just purely for information but also for relationships and the ability to give us advice. AI devices will be able to provide counsel using data like never before. Their assistance to the human race will be limitless. The key is that we have to make things right before we get super intelligent and superhuman machines. Therefore, we ought to keep our definition of AI simple, altruistic, uncertain of our objectives. We ought to also have the ability to learn more by observing all humans.

Case Study

Frank is a researcher working in a company in Cambridge, MA. He loves educating people about AI, but he knows that there is a lot of prejudice against the types of machines that a person may come across. He longs to tell everyone what AI promises for the human race. In a presentation at his company, he made the following remarks, "I think it is important for us to realize that the realignment of human values with AI will be the essential task we can undertake for the next generation of robots. Like Stewart Russell, I think that we must see how robots stand to benefit the human race because they will never be able to think for themselves and what is good for their own race. As long as we keep building machines, we can only think of how they will best serve humanity and its purposes. Therefore, stop worrying about the future and what humans could do in a dystopian environment. 1984 is not going to happen anytime soon. Don't think that machines can take over the world. They can only do so with human intervention. That's the only way, but I'm sure that we're always going to keep our best interests in mind."

Conclusion

To sum it all up, it is clear that we have some methods in place that can protect the human race and create an AI that is safe for use, but we must always keep in mind our own objectives, which the robots will always be uncertain of and will continually require programming to access that information. We can only give a certain amount of information to the robot. They will not seek their own initiative because we have not programmed them to be able to do that. Most AI researchers and engineers are mindful of this aspect and therefore, will only focus on the good of humanity in the design of robots that are intended for use by humans. Therefore, we can be secure in knowing that the robots will be able to obey all the commands that we set out to give them and will not act in their own autonomy or will. No need to fear, our future is safe and can be influenced continually by our human will and motivation.

Chapter : 6
How to Create an AI Ready Culture

"Compassionate Artificial Intelligence can transform and heal the world from a much deeper sense. They can add values and transform our world, our families, our workplaces, and our communities."

— Amit Ray, Compassionate Artificial Intelligence (Artificial Intelligence, Good Reads)

How can we ensure that our companies are prepared for AI and can bring about a successful transformation that could lead to significant gains and profits?

One important aspect is recognizing that our decisions are made best through data and evidence rather than the opinions of people (Khurana, 2017). When we collect more data about a topic, then we can make better decisions. Therefore, we must continuously learn about the data that we collect. Our working environments continue to change and are fluid and dynamic. Every day, we must challenge, validate, and adapt our models. Additionally, our basic assumptions and models can develop over time, so we have to re-learn information frequently to maintain momentum and keep up with the times. We can use new information to strengthen our companies and decentralize the making of decisions by management (Khurana, 2017).

As we recognize the ability to make AI part of our organizations, we should take a look at several steps to follow.

1   Create a Culture of Evidence-based Decisions in Your Organization

The first thing we need to do is to realize that the best decisions are made by empirical evidence and not the subjectivity of humans (Khurana, 2017). Too many of us place importance on following the advice of senior officials in our organization, who have more experience than us. They know the market well and have been through various periods in the company's history. However, would you rather listen to someone's opinion or the facts themselves? In today's working world, objectivity is a crucial aspect of what we do in the office.

2   Always Monitor, Test, and Course-Correct

Today's data world can be ambiguous and difficult to test. Furthermore, our decisions can be prone to error. We need to do a lot of course corrections to help us steer clear of making crucial mistakes. Our organizations must be flexible to monitor the progress of work and correct the course, if necessary.

3   Measure and Record All Transactions

Next, we need to have all the data to make our decisions, so we need to measure and record all the details of our lives. We should capture data as much as possible. The good idea is to monitor assets that cost more than $20. By allowing systems to capture the data, then we can model, optimize, and train AI (Khurana, 2017).

4   Digitally connect the extended organization and enable information workflow

Connecting ourselves digitally is an important step to making an AI-ready work culture. The sooner we can create a digital space to store all of our work information, whether that is in the cloud or on Google Drive, the sooner, we can make great things happen in our organizations.

5   Empower Employees to Make Decisions

The next step is decentralizing the decision-making and giving employees the power to make their own decisions based on data collection. As we advance, we realize the need to break down the hierarchical structures, which are antiquated and inefficient. By giving employees more autonomy by making fact-based choices, then we are effectively allowing them to be the center of the organization.

6   Using AI as a systematic process with a measurable impact (Khurana, 2017).

As we design the AI, we can use them to have an impact on our societies and organizations. The more emphasis we put on their benefits, the greater advantages we will experience in the implementation of AI technology in our workplaces.

7   Diversify the Set of Knowledge of the Workers

Another important aspect of preparing workers for AI is to diversify skillsets. With AI's ongoing contributions to the workplace, it becomes crucial for workers to follow suit and update their skills and knowledge to fit with the fact that AI will replace, generate, and develop our work and jobs. Having an entire company on board will help everyone to keep up the pace with the latest developments in technology.

8   Introduce-AI training and Continuous Learning

Next, we need to introduce AI-training courses and continuous learning, which will get all workers familiar with AI technology. Today and tomorrow's AI-infused workplace will require training and learning that will help workers to update their existing knowledge and skills, specifically about AI (Forbes, 2019).

9 Engage the Workplace with Technology Consultants

After introducing AI-training courses, we also need to have the support of people, who are trained in AI and can help us update our existing courses to match with the current industry and ensure that everything works in our favor and our companies are well-informed. By networking with the top AI talent, then we can be assured of future success.

10 Create incentives for people who are making progress in AI leadership

Finally, it is important to create incentives, bonuses, and other benefits for people who are constantly engaging with AI in our organizations (Forbes, 2019). The more perks we provide, the more we will see people interested in this topic which will benefit the organization at hand.

Case Study

Ashley and Pierre were working for an organization in Boston, which specializes in automated technology. They realized that they needed more training for it, so the organization provided them with a course that would refresh their memory of what automated technology is, as well as give them the support to be able to do this work. It was crucial that they get informed about the latest developments in the world of technology. That was a key aspect of the mission of the company. With this investment in training, new professionals were getting raises and benefits that would provide them with new reasons to pursue the research and development of AI technology.

Conclusion

As the workplace becomes more saturated with AI technology, it is important to prepare for the future. We don't know exactly what the world will look like in ten years. By 2030, AI will have an important place in the world economy. The more prepared we are to face the challenges of AI, the better our work will be. Therefore, it is crucial that we don't get left in the dust because the implementation of AI technology is going to continue to be an integral part of future developments in the global workplace.

Chapter : 7
Investing in Technical Talent

"You need to remember that the technology doesn't get to decide; it is humans that get to decide. Human beings make technology."

-Will.I.AM, Rapper, Producer, and Philanthropist (The Mission, 2018)

If we are to increase the role of AI in our workplaces, it is important for us to put the emphasis not just on the technology but on the people, who will use their skills to promote it. Groopman wrote in the Entrepreneur Asia Pacific how investing in people needs to be at the forefront of our priorities, as much as it is on the data that we collect.

Investing in People Not Just Machines

Investment in AI includes people that do not just have technical talent. We want to also target people in the following fields: product leaders, front-line associates, subject matter experts, designers, sales associates, leaders, end-users, data scientists, and technical builders. As we target such individuals, we have the task of educating people and calming their fears about the future, as well as preparing future stakeholders (Groopman, 2018). Another task is to equip these agents with knowledge, tools, and the confidence to sell AI and receive incentives for doing so.

As we develop new teams with technical talent, we must cultivate an environment with people who want to deal with AI's cultural stigma and people's unwillingness to work for the cause of AI. Paradoxically, the key to the success of AI is the people's willingness to work with it (Groopman, 2018).

Undoubtedly, there will be problems with the advancement of AI, which includes job displacement, algorithmic bias, privacy and surveillance, and security threats. Additionally, the dangers of autonomous machines and manipulation of data and AI loom, as well as the notion of killer robots. All of these fears are valid. What needs to be done is building an AI mindset that dispels the myths and provides a progressive view of AI.

One way of building an AI mindset includes involving employees in the design of AI, which will speed up the process, increase savings and revenues, among other things. AI must be developed by people who possess different sets of skills. People who are responsible for the day to day workflow can understand how breakdowns happen and what to do when the product fails to deliver what is promised, as well as where the customer's sensitivities are (Groopman, 2018). It is vital that we find people who are willing to deal with the challenges of AI and provide products that are worth investing in because they help people find solutions to society's problems.

Case Study

James was fascinated by all aspects of AI. He had researched the topic since he was a young child, and to this day, he still continues to do research on AI. Although he was so enthralled by AI, he knew that what was required to make it all happen was human resources. The people who are responsible for designing these machines are essential to the important aspects of AI development. People should not think that it's all about the machines, as much as it is about the creators and innovators, who are at the forefront of cutting-edge research happening every day in labs across the country. As a manager for a research think tank, James knew that he had to motivate people to join his team, who were forward thinking and driven toward human progress. It was not enough to emphasize the devices and what they do. What was even more important was how to attract top talent to work on the most high-profile research on AI. With that mindset, James continued to recruit people who wanted to design sophisticated and original designs.

Conclusion

It is necessary to view the issue of AI as something that is to be solved collectively by society with different ranges of talent. That doesn't just include the scientists and engineers of AI, but rather it includes all different types of technical and nontechnical talent, which can contribute to AI. It is not enough to say that the current AI researchers can be the only ones involved in the process. We need to involve many different kinds of people with different inputs, valuable skill sets, and opinions, which can influence a new generation of AI technology. This is the only way that we can move forward and achieve the results that we desire in our AI developments. Manpower is to be the center of all that we do because human progress is the way of the future.

Chapter : 8
Plan Your Implementation

"The greatest benefit of the arrival of artificial intelligence is that AIs will help define humanity. We need AIs to tell us who we are."

– Kevin Kelly (Brown, 2019)

Artificial intelligence has become a big business buzzword today, and more businesses are keen on implementing it in their marketing strategies. AI and machine learning are continually evolving, just as companies are building their approaches to these new technologies (Ross, 2018).

Forrester recently said that two-thirds of business technology decision-makers have either implemented are in the process of implementing, or are expanding their range and usage of AI. Businesses are set to spend over 47 billion dollars in 2020 on AI technologies, which is up from 8 billion dollars in 2016 (Ross, 2018).

Over the next several years, organizations in different sectors of the economy will continue to support the development of AI and machine learning. This will transform their core operations and business models to include machine learning systems, which will greatly improve their functions and create cost-effective strategies for their operation. As business leaders chart out their plans to use AI, it is important to keep in mind that getting to an AI-ready marketplace is a journey and not a destination. Therefore, each organization should carefully consider implementing AI by following several steps (Ross, 2018).

1   Define When Technology Will be Used

The first thing that businesses need to consider is how they will use AI to solve their unique problems and challenges (Ross, 2018). If they have a specific goal in mind, then they will have more success in implementing AI. Stating that a company wants to increase its online sales by 20% is not a specific goal. To make this more specific, you could add that you want to increase sales by 20% by monitoring the demographics of website visitors. That can be better understood by people who are investing in the company.

2   Make sure that there is available data

After defining how technology will be used, you should ensure that you can collect data, which can be analyzed and used for business purposes. A lot of work time is spent taking in data, so it is important that businesses understand how to get the right data in sufficient volumes. It's important to note that quality data is crucial to successful business strategies and outcomes (Ross, 2018).

3   Do Some Basic Data Exploration

After this process, it is important to do some basic data exploration to make sure the data is telling the right story, based on the organization's business model and structure.

4   Define a Model-Building Method to Use

Instead of thinking about the destination and end objective, it is important to think about the hypothesis itself. By doing tests to determine what variables or features are the most important, you can then figure out how to use your hypothesis to produce results. Business experts need to be involved in this process because they must give feedback to ensure that everyone is on the same page (Ross, 2018).

5   Create a Model that Validates the Method

When we define performance measures, we will need to use a model that validates the method that we have used. The model will be used in the involved data analysis.

6   Automation and Product Roll-out

After the model has been created and validated, it needs to go to the assembly line for production. The product will roll-out for a few weeks, and then the model will be tested and evaluated during its beginning stages. The correct tools need to be chosen to complete automation on data collection, with systems that have been implemented in order to share results with the right audiences. The platform used in this process needs to include varying interfaces, which are marked for the varying levels of knowledge of the organization's AI technology by different users (Ross, 2018).

7   Continuously Update the Model

As soon as you have created your model, then you must continuously monitor it and assess its validity. Then, you can update the model as needed.

Models may become out of date for different reasons. Market dynamics, or the business model, can change over time. Models are designed based on predictions of future outcomes, using past data. As market dynamics shift away from the company's business practices, then the model becomes irrelevant and in need of updates (Ross, 2018).

Case Study

Terry was working for a company that was experimenting with AI, but it was not yet using the technology. The company was located in Kansas, out in the middle of nowhere. Unfortunately, this company's mentality was stuck in 1990, so employers didn't want to try out new technological advances. Furthermore, people were not inclined to use AI technology. As work started to pile up and administrative tasks became heavier for people, it became clear that something needed to be done. Terry advocated for AI implementation to streamline the administrative tasks using a plug-in software, which could help the members of the team to complete administrative tasks using AI. Pretty soon, the company started to use AI in conjunction with human agents to complete data entry and collection, as well as scheduling events. In the end, everyone's life became simpler and more enhanced because of the role AI technology had in the company. See, it isn't so awful after all.

Conclusion

It is evident that in order to plan the effective implementation of AI, you need to develop a good model, which is constantly evolving to fit the unique market dynamics. If a business model remains in the past, then it will not move forward, and the business will likely not succeed. By implementing a good model, the company can use new information on markets to update their model to fit with advancing AI technology.

Chapter : 9
Collect and Prepare Data

"Part of our wishlist for our lives and our future should be disentangling wisdom from intelligence. In our era of Big Data and algorithms, they're easy to conflate."

– Arianna Huffington, Founder of the Huffington Post (VPUE Identity Guidelines, Stanford)

With current advancements in AI technology, machine learning has continually been related in some way to AI. Many people think that machine learning is artificial intelligence. The truth is that machine learning is a small part of artificial intelligence. It is a discipline, which relies on data collection to perform both supervised or unsupervised AI training (Chan, n.d.).

In both supervised and unsupervised learning, the important thing is to collect quality data. The process which requires the most time is preparing data that is needed to train the machine. Brian Ka Chan talks about how data preparation comprises 80% of his team's time. Preparing data requires the following steps (n.d.):

1. Identify the required data
2. Identify the availability and location of the data
3. Profiling the data
4. Sourcing the data
5. Integration of data
6. Cleansing the data
7. Preparing the data for learning

These seven steps are important because they determine whether a machine learning process will be successful or not.

Practice Mindful Data Collection

Chan talks about how the best way to avoid failure in machine learning is to practice mindful AI data collection. He defines this as the practice of thinking about the use of data before they are created for your business or activity. In most cases, you generate data in your workspace for transactional purposes only. Data is generated because we should complete some kind of transaction, so we define the data on our terms. However, mindful data goes beyond that step. A mindful data collector thinks about whether data points already exist within a business (Chan, n.d.).

If a data point already exists in a business, then it is better to leverage metadata and modify it rather than starting from ground zero. To practice effective mindful data collection, here are some things you can do (Chan, n.d.):

1 Look through a current data dictionary
2 Assess your data governance organization
3 Check on the administrators of major processes within your company
4 Review standards of data collection and usage

Regulating Data Quality

Mindful data collection in AI also requires a high-quality set of data. There are three different factors that influence data quality, including data quality requirements, data rules, and data policies. Many companies use data quality as a strategy to manage their employees. About 80% of the time spent on data science projects is spent performing data cleansing and management. But if you have mindful data quality, then you can shorten that time by about half.

Think about the amount of money you can save by being more mindful rather than investing in invoices from expert engineers, who know a lot about data science and machine learning. Also, think about the flexibility your team will have if you reduce the time in the data processing phase (Chan, n.d.).

Conclusion

Data collection is not meant to be a mindless exercise of futility that many people make it into different companies. Many times, we don't want to perform data collection. But it is a necessary part of our lives in business. Data collection is something that takes an inordinate amount of time to complete, but it must be done to promote an equitable future. Mindful data collection helps you to carefully sift through the collection of data and extract the most valuable information. When you can combine data collection with the use of AI, then you can increase value to your company and bring in good returns. AI will also help your company reduce the risk of making mistakes while ensuring that the data is properly collected and analyzed. Finally, invest in data collection to secure your company in the future.

Chapter : 10
Build Machine Learning Models

"There is no reason and no way that a human mind can keep up with an Intelligent artificial machine by 2035."

– Gray Scott (Brown, 2019)

In this chapter, we will talk about how to build machine learning models from scratch. There will be a lot of important concepts needing an explanation, which can help you to understand how to develop the model fully.

    1   Define the Problem that is Involved

The first and most important thing that you need to do is find out what the inputs and outputs are (Roman, 2018). You must answer the following questions:

    a. What is the objective we're trying to achieve?
    b. What do we want to predict is going to happen?
    c. What are the features desired?
    d. What is the input data?
    e. What is the expected level of improvement?

Not every issue can be resolved until we have a model, so we can make some hypotheses based on given information.

It is important to recognize that machine learning can only be used to memorize patterns that have been used before. We use machine learning, assuming that future patterns will resemble what has been experienced in the past. However, this is not consistently true.

2 Collect Data

Data collection is one of the first steps in developing machine learning. This will help evaluate the quality of the model. Once we have developed a good model, then we will get better data, and our model will improve its performance.

3 Choose a Measure of Success

Peter Drucker, Harvard professor, said, "If you can't measure it, you can't improve it" (Roman, 2018). If you want to control something, then you need to observe it and measure it. You need to have precision and accuracy to achieve your goal.

The measure should be related to the goals of the business and should be used to address any problem we are facing. For example, regression problems use evaluation metrics such as mean squared error (MSE) and classification problems might use evaluation metrics, such as precision, recall, and accuracy (Roman, 2018).

4 Prepare the Data

Before you begin to train models, you need to transform the data so that it can be put into the machine learning model (Roman, 2018). For example:

a. Dealing with missing data

Today, we always see missing data values, which may be due to errors in the data collection or blank spaces in surveys, among other items.

b. Handle categorical data

When we deal with categorical data, we must use ordinal and nominal features. Ordinal features can be sorted and ordered.

However, nominal features do not require a specific order. We can deal with these issues by mapping ordinal features and encoding nominal class labels.

    c.   Feature scaling

The next step in this process is feature scaling. The majority of machine learning algorithms function optimally when the features they use are on the same scale. The way to do this includes normalization and standardization.

    d. Selecting meaningful features
    e. Split the data into three parts, including training, testing, and validating sets. We can train our model using training data, evaluate it based on validation data, and then test it on the test data that we use.
    5   Developing a Benchmark Model

The fifth step in this process involves developing a benchmark model that serves as a basic component on which we can measure the performance of an algorithm.

    6   Develop a Better Model that Has Improved Parameters

Finally, you should take your model and make it into the best possible one that can help your company grow.

Conclusion

To have a good AI structure, you need to develop a good model to follow and carry out all the functions of your business. AI requires utmost dedication. Creating a model involves developing a plan of action, where you can solve a given problem. The sooner you have developed a good strategy for handling the problem, and then you can collect data and prepare it to create the benchmark model, which is helpful to integrate into your company. You must have a willingness to take risks, develop a growth mindset, and take on responsibilities of equipping your workforce for AI. Developing models takes time and energy, but it is well worth it to create your AI-ready task force.

Chapter : 11
Experiment and Iterate

"The ultimate search engine, which would understand, you know, exactly what you wanted when you typed in a query, and it would give you the exact right thing back, in computer science we call that artificial intelligence. That means it would be smart, and we're a long way from having smart computers."

– Larry Page (Brown, 2019)

This chapter will explore the different experiments that you can carry out while you discover more about machine learning.

Because machine learning and artificial intelligence can be difficult concepts for the average person to take in, developers are creating demos of their content so that everyone can be more aware. The following fun AI experiments can be explored online. They involved the use of pictures, music, drawings, and more.

Let's look at a collection of the best AI experiments that will get you started.

AttnGAN- Image generation machine

In 2018, AI research and development teams from Microsoft's Deep Learning Technology Center created an algorithm that can visualize text-based captions. When the researchers taught the AI about images and visualizations, they used cat images exclusively, and it was able to produce some interesting results. However, when the AI was trained using more diverse images, it became overwhelmed with information (Morikawa, 2018).

AI Duet- Playing Piano with an AI

If you don't have a partner to play with you, then you can play the piano with Google's Creative Lab piano. It responds back to you. You can simply enter in some notes, and the machine will create your melody (Morikawa, 2018).

pix2pix- Image to Image translation

Using an interactive demo, you can make your line drawings into fantastic works of art. You can sketch your simple drawing and watch as the pix2pix AI automatically re-creates your drawing into dogs, buildings, or clothing (Morikawa, 2018). This device has been trained on different images, and it attempts to create the corresponding output image with any input image that is given to it.

Shelley AI- Human-AI collaboration to make horror stories

This AI was trained with creepy stories. AI-based horror fiction author Shelley has been writing horror stories using Twitter since 2017. Shelley uses Twitter and uses lines from Tweets to generate a story and provide a twist of her own.

FastPhotoStyle- Photo Style Transfer

This AI uses an algorithm that can use the style taken from a digital image or photo and make it into a totally different one, which creates unique results.

Thing Translator

The Thing Translator is a fun device to use because you can simply walk around an office and scan items to find instant translations that it provides into nine languages (Phillips, 2017). It has an addictive quality to it. The Thing Translator cannot translate absolutely everything it sees, but it tries to translate whatever you put in front of it. If it recognizes something, it will default to saying "image" or "design."

With a Thing Translator, you might run into some interesting situations. For example, one user took a picture of his face and received the response, "hair." This was pretty interesting, given that he had a beard, but it was not the words "face" or "boy/man" that he was expecting.

One user's kids would point it at a rug and expect it to say "rug" or "carpet," but instead, the device produced the word, "crochet."

Thing Translator is not a completely fool-proof device, but it could help a person who is traveling from company to company and to different countries. To use the Thing Translator, you need to have an Android smartphone with a camera or a PC with a camera. It is currently not available for users with Apple devices.

It is apparent that AI has many practical uses, and you can have fun and play with it. AI is meant to be enjoyed as well as used for practical purposes. There are a wide variety of options that AI can provide for your company. You can enjoy it at home, as well. With all the entertaining features of AI, it's easy to experiment with it and determine which AI will bring revenue to your business.

Case Study

Suzannah used Amazon to buy all of her purchases for her home and family. She would buy anything from books, home supplies, cookware, and everything else. Little did she know, Amazon was using AI technology to figure out what she wanted to buy. The AI that Amazon uses helps drive algorithms, which promote its marketing strategy. Therefore, Amazon can predict what products will be demanded by its customers and gives recommendations based on customer searches. Additionally, these searches help promote their sales.

Later, Suzannah went through her recommendation feed and found a limited-edition cookbook by Martha Stewart. She could not believe that Amazon was advertising it; however, it had used previous information that she had typed in the computer to come up with the product suggestion. Having already researched Martha Stewart Living, and other related searches, the computer knew that Suzannah wanted this cookbook.

The implications for businesses include the readying of companies for technology that can boost sales and can give them a boost in opportunities to gain new clientele. The Internet has made it simpler to be able to do this and allows you to find any product you want, simply by looking on the Internet. Companies can use this information to market their products well.

Case Study #2: eBay

eBay has been using machine learning as a way to promote its business strategy. eBay's AI, Shopbot, enables users to find products that they are interested in with ease. Already, customers are able to communicate with the automated assistant with text, voice, or pictures that have been taken from their phones. This is a case in which people are able to experiment with and use technology to buy what they want online. It is incredible how close we are getting to using AI in every aspect of our daily lives. Many people spend countless hours shopping online. This is one of the ways that they can use AI to benefit their lives.

Businesses can adopt the AI model that is used by eBay, which is an automated customer service that people can access anywhere 24/7 and 365 days a year. Through using these services, customers will be well-served and able to do many things. This is the future of AI services for businesses.

Conclusion

It is important to experiment with the possibilities of what AI can do for your business. There are many developments that make AI a winning solution for your company. You have to play with it a little bit and see if it can help you and your company. Take a look at it and discover the different features of AI that you can implement in your business. The only way you'll know if it works is if you find the right solution. But that takes a lot of trial and error. You won't find the solution overnight, but if you can try different things, you should be able to find something that works for your business, and which will advance your marketing strategies and salesforce.

Chapter : 12
Obstacles and Opportunities

"Technology is going to disrupt the future of work, perhaps sooner than we thought. We are exploring everything from AI to VR, but we see no substitute for our stores and our employees. We focus on building talent and personal service."

— Brian Cornell, Board Chairman, CEO, Target at NRF 2019 (Skorupa, 2019).

This chapter will explore the unique challenges and opportunities that we are confronted with as we use AI every day.

Because humans and machines are collaborating more closely now than ever before, AI is no longer going to remain in the labs of highly skilled technicians. Instead, it is providing amazing possibilities for our country's future (Mehta, 2018).

AI continues to give rise to both inspiration and deep skepticism but in different ways. Although there continues to be a societal prejudice against it, businesses must recognize the need to overcome challenges before they can recognize the real potential of this technology. What we have to do is maximize the opportunities to use the AI.

Proof: Why Does it Work?

Organizations that are developing AI often cannot prove exactly why AI does what it does. So, it makes people intensely skeptical of it. Proving the validity of AI remains a difficult thing for organizations to do. Therefore, what organizations need to do is to make AI easily explainable, provable, and transparent. They must use explainable AI as their main source of teaching and learning.

Privacy

Many AI applications use a large amount of data to learn and make decisions. Machine learning systems are incorporating data that includes personal information, making it vulnerable to attacks, such as data breach or identity theft. Consequently, the European Union has chosen to propose the General Data Protection Regulation to help with the protection of personal information (Mehta, 2018).

Solution: To confront this challenge, data scientists are working together to develop AI using Federated Learning in such a way that they won't compromise user data.

Problem: Algorithm Bias

One of the problems faced by AI systems is that there are certain biases that underlie the data on which they operate. Data may include ethnic, racial, gender, and other biases. Algorithms might identify who gets a job interview, who gets a loan, among other things. Google Photos helps people to identify people, objects, and scenes. But it is possible that it can show the unintended results, including when there are racial biases in the camera roll (Mehta, 2018).

Future predictions show that biases will continue to be a part of AI systems, including bad data. But it is important that we train them with unbiased data and develop algorithms that can be explained easily to others. Microsoft is developing a tool that will help identify algorithm bias. This is a very important part of helping to identify unfairness in machine learning. It will be a great opportunity for businesses to use AI so as to not discriminate against a select group of people.

A person within a business could use an approach like "Path Specific Counterfactual Fairness" by DeepMind researchers to get rid of the biases (Mehta, 2018).

Data Scarcity

With more data coming in than ever before, there are still rare sets of applicable data useful for training AI. The most powerful AI machines that are on the planet are ones that use supervised learning, which requires labeled data. These data sets allow the machines to learn with the digestible bits of information. However, labeled data is short in supply. In the future, we might also have very complex algorithms, which are generated by deep learning, which will exacerbate this problem (Mehta, 2018).

Solution

Organizations continue to invest in design methodologies, which will help them find out how to make AI models learn without the abundance of labeled data. The way forward is learning how to interpret these numbers and the relationships within them. The future belongs to organizations, which can help improve the capabilities of AI devices and use human creativity and judgment to design them.

Trust Issues

At the heart of all AI, there is a technical side, which is based on science and algorithms that can get pretty complicated. People who don't understand these things will have a hard time trying to relate to the information. At the heart of human beings is a desire to make things simple. Often, we overlook things that we cannot understand and tend to stay away from anything that might cause us trouble. Because AI uses large quantities of extraneous data, many users cannot grasp these concepts (Lath, 2018).

AI Human Interaction

With the challenge of humans that cannot understand the concepts of AI, there is a shortage of people who have advanced skills in AI. Therefore, businesses must train their professionals to understand what the benefits are to AI technology. Many people think that the biggest challenge to AI is accepting the fact that workflow dynamics change and jobs will change, as a result of AI implementation. Therefore, they are understandably cautious about moving forward.

Lack of Investment

Another challenge that many people are facing is a lack of investment by different managers. AI implementation is expensive and requires a lot of start-up money before a business will be able to see a return on their investment. Not every business owner will be able to invest in technology (Lath, 2018).

Software Malfunction

Technology can fail us at any time. One minute you're sitting playing on your computer and another minute, the screen is frozen, and you cannot close any open windows. Then soon, the computer automatically shuts down, and you lose all of your data. Technology has the ability to do things that we cannot understand. And when something does go wrong, it can be difficult for us to know exactly what happened. Whereas, when a human performs a task, and something goes wrong, we can trace the act and know who is responsible.

When machines and algorithms are considered, it is difficult to point fingers at the technology, especially when trying to find the cause of a computer glitch or crash. One example of AI going wrong is when a self-driving car killed a pedestrian (Lath, 2018).

AI Cannot Be the Replacement for Everything

Since the beginning of AI, we may have thought that fancy technology could be used in place of every single task or experience in our lives. With the Hollywoodish fantasies of AI technology, we think that this could totally happen. While it is true that AI will play a great role in our lives, not every task can be performed by AI.

AI is a tool that increases your productivity. It can replace all kinds of tasks to make you more productive with your time. It allows you to perform at your best and increase the efficiency of your work.

Failure to Meet Unreasonable Expectations

With many people, there is a problem with unmet expectations. People who don't know about the intricacies of AI may develop unreasonable expectations of what AI can do, while not understanding what its true capabilities are. As humans, we tend to think of AI in romantic terms and in ways that will make it excellent and beneficial. However, there are limitations to how much this technology can be used to further the advancement of humanity.

Many people are saying that artificial intelligence will reign supreme in the coming era, but there are many challenges that will be encountered by AI (Lath, 2018). Although still in its initial phases, AI will continue to grow and develop.

Case Study

Steve was an entrepreneur who had designed his own business. He started it all from scratch and started out with a few people who were in his online music company. Steve was really interested in AI, although he didn't fully understand it. He wanted to learn more and educate himself about AI. However, he still had grandiose and romantic associations with AI and how it could grow his business. Moreover, he thought that he could make a ton of money simply by buying some AI technology to take care of automated customer service and making money on ads through his music service that he created. However, it turns out that he was not able to make as much money as he had expected. Additionally, there were limits to his start-up in terms of how much he could invest in AI. All the fancy features that he had imagined using were not yet invented or would be extremely expensive and out of his price range. Therefore, Steve was setting himself up for disappointment and potential failures with his business, due to unreasonable expectations of what AI could do for him and his business.

Conclusion

We have to be reasonable with AI. It's not the cure-all or savior of the universe. Instead, it is a tool that we can use in our businesses to grow our revenue and attract new customers. It is expensive to invest in AI technology, and there are continuous limits to what can be developed because we are not fifty years in the future. Instead, we are still in the beginning phases of full implementation into a business. If you can remember, twenty-five years ago, people were just getting into using computers. In the beginning, they were super expensive, low functioning, and huge. Fast forward to the present day, and you have technology that is lighter, portable, and more powerful than ever. Now we use a smartphone as our computer, phone, and music device. There is a lot we can do as we wait for AI to take its place as a replacement for many tasks, devices, and jobs. However, it will come in the near future.

Chapter : 13
General and Administrative

"It's likely that machines will be smarter than us before the end of the century—not just at chess or trivia questions but at just about everything, from mathematics and engineering to science and medicine."

– Gary Marcus (Rosso, 2018)

In this chapter, we will talk about how AI will change the face of the administration in businesses worldwide.

Many people have said that artificial intelligence is going to uproot the workforce and cause people to lose their jobs, especially those who hold jobs that are easy-to-automate. Managers of companies around the world will have to contend with the increased intervention of AI technology. The truth is that AI will soon have the capacity to complete all of the administrative tasks that will save managers time and money (Kolbjornsrud, Amico, & Thomas, 2016).

How can managers use the information of AI to develop and grow their business? A Harvard Business School survey of 1,770 managers, from 14 countries and with 37 interviews, reveals the best practices that successful managers will need to understand and use in this advanced digital age (Kolbjornsrud, Amico, & Thomas, 2016).

Let AI do all the Admin Work

The survey showed that managers from different backgrounds spend more than 50% of their time on administrative tasks. For example, a restaurant manager or lead doctor at a hospital must continually work around the shift schedule because of his or her team's sick leave, turnover, or departure. These are tasks that can be easily automated to help out the team (Kolbjornsrud, Amico, & Thomas, 2016).

Report writing is another example. The Associated Press expanded its reporting from 300 stories to 4,400 using AI-powered robots, which would write reports. Using this technology, journalists were free to pursue more detailed and interpretive reporting. Imagine that you manage a small business or company. You may have to draft your latest management report. However, technology could do it for you. It is already possible for technology to make an analytical and statistical report of information. Another example of how this works is the recent partnership between the data analytics company Tableau and Narrative Science, which was intended to help develop language generation tools. As a result of this collaboration, a Chrome extension was developed to automatically generate and report explanations for Tableau graphics (Kolbjornsrud, Amico, & Thomas, 2016).

Managers from this survey felt the positivity of this development. The vast majority of managers want to have support with both monitoring and reporting.

Focus on Judgment Work

There are many decisions that must be made that don't include the help of a machine. Managers must use their knowledge of the company and provide empathy and ethical reflection on different matters. And what is needed most is human judgment, because it applies experience and training to the most important business practices and decisions. With judgment, further talents must be applied, including creative and out-of-the-box thinking, experimentation, data analysis, and development of strategies, which enable a business to flourish in the future.

Many managers think that every decision they make requires judgment, experience, and skills that don't need machines. But what if machines have the ability to facilitate those judgments and make those decisions? Then, we would have a good combination between the manager and the machine. AI devices were never meant to replace managers and their essential role in business, but rather to complement them.

Call Your Intelligent Machine Your Colleague

When a machine is viewed as an equal rather than a rival, then it opens up the door to more trust in the world of AI. Although human judgment is likely not to be automated, intelligent machines can provide a lot to our decision-making processes, as well as our ability to search for information. According to one survey, 78% of managers think that they will trust the advice of AI systems in making their business decisions in future transactions (Kolbjornsrud, Amico, & Thomas, 2016).

Kensho Technologies, a company that focuses on analytics, asks the hard questions about investment in machines to help managers make decisions and explore different business situations (Kolbjornsrud, Amico, & Thomas, 2016).

AI has the capacity to increase the workload of managers while also allowing managers to get more done. But there is an increased ability to interact with machines in such a way that the manager always has a personal assistant available 24/7/365 to help with whatever task needs to be done.

Use Creative Powers to Get Things Done

Managers today think that they need to develop their creative thinking skills so they can remain successful in the usage and implementation of AI. Managers also operate like designers in that they design complex road-maps and implement ideas to be carried out.

In an age when more things need to be done creatively and with a good attitude, fostering your inner creative genius will help you to get a lot more done and get you on the right track (Kolbjornsrud, Amico, & Thomas, 2016).

While the AI is doing the Admin, You Do the "Social" Work

While the AI carries out all the many administrative and analytical work, the manager can do all the work that involves social skills, including networking, coaching, and collaborating. Although managers will have to use technology to understand the knowledge and judgment of their customers and online communities, they must also bring together the wide variety of talents and insights of their colleagues and contacts, because this will help them to make the most informed decisions for their company.

How Your Company Can Be More Successful with AI

When people start using AI, they will realize how much cheaper, more impartial, and more efficient machines can be in carrying out actions and jobs. Although machines may have the power to outperform humans at these various tasks,

71

managers don't need to be worried or alarmed. Instead, they can focus on the things that only humans can do and remain intent on solving their company's problems.

A machine can definitely write a report, which would take a human a lot of time. But engaging with a team and providing motivation and support is something only a human being can provide. Time-tabling and doing other things may become a thing managed by machines but providing strategy and vision for the future is only something that a human can do. Therefore, it is crucial that we adopt a means to use AI in our administrative tasks and leave the judgment calls to the human. That will be the most successful thing we can do for our sustainable future (Kolbjornsrud, Amico, & Thomas, 2016).

What Managers Must do with AI

To facilitate a smooth implementation of AI technology, managers need to experiment with it in using it for their purposes. They need to also put everyone in the organization on board with using it to further the objectives for the organization. Additionally, managers should try to develop strategies to recruit creative, collaborative, and empathetic team members, who can provide experience and emotional intelligence, which will allow everyone to support one another. They should have a "we're in this together" mentality, which will be helpful in advancing and getting them off their feet.

Case Study

Jessica was an entrepreneur who had started her own business in marketing. She was a successful and proud CEO who loved every aspect of what she did. But she realized that she was running out of manpower to be able to handle the daily managerial tasks that she had. Her workforce quickly surged to more than 50 workers, which was more than she had before. Jessica became quickly overwhelmed with how to schedule various activities in her business. The day-to-day admin work became more than a hassle for her as she was spending more than 75% of her time on this task. It was draining her emotionally and physically. Then, she researched about using AI devices to help with managing her workload and found that she was able to reduce her work by more than 50% significantly. Her virtual assistant Bob became an important part of her daily work routine. Every day, she would consult Bob and have him manage her personal schedule, as well as that of her co-workers and associates. It helped her a lot. Pretty soon, Jessica was relying on this technology for all the important admin work and phased out her previous work. As a result, she was able to focus on building relationships with her key players and making important business contacts to grow her business.

Conclusion

There are some tasks that people dread performing, including data entry, schedule-making, and other administrative tasks. These are things that can be done efficiently by machines, which can do great work. Indeed, machine learning has enabled AI devices to learn how to do these basic tasks automatically. Administrative tasks can be susceptible to human error because of basic calculation mistakes. However, when an AI device enters the picture, then the job becomes much easier for the human to tackle. They can defer to the machine to complete the job at the same level and capacity of a human being. However, this will not entirely replace the need for administrative assistants and workers. There is always a social and relational aspect to work that can only be carried out by human beings. Machines will never be able to match this level of interpersonal relationships and emotional intelligence. Conversely, when humans don't have their hands tied up with a lot of difficult, tedious, and monotonous work, then they are free to pursue relationships with one another, which makes the job a lot easier and more efficient.

Chapter : 14
Human Resources and Talent

"I have always been convinced that the only way to get artificial intelligence to work is to do the computation in a way similar to the human brain. That is the goal I have been pursuing. We are making progress, though we still have lots to learn about how the brain actually works."

– Geoffrey Hinton (Rosso, 2018)

The future of HR is about to become a reality with digital advancements, which will maximize the possibility of human and automated collaboration. This is making a new priority for HR, which requires business leaders and teams to become fluent in the language of artificial intelligence so they can see HR as something that is more personal, interactive, and human than ever before. Here are some trends that HR should prepare for as artificial intelligence begins to make its mark on the recruitment of teams (Meister, 2019).

AI and Human Intelligence= An Interactive Candidate Experience

Many teams rely on AI to help in talent acquisition, which can reduce the time that is needed to hire key people. AI allows teams to make for a simple recruitment experience that is highly effective.

Case Study #1

One company has been able to use AI in its recruitment. The company's name is DBS Bank, which created JIM, a virtual recruitment bot, which would be used to screen out candidates for a high-volume job position in the consumer bank. After JIM was introduced to the company, the time spent on screening applications was reduced from 32 minutes to 8 minutes. More job application screenings were completed because of this wizard. Additionally, the team was able to communicate more effectively with their candidates.

The key takeaway from this experience is that recruiters no longer have to spend thousands of hours screening applicants in high volume jobs. Instead, they are free to pursue higher-value work, which includes recruitment, marketing, and engaging with the candidates on a personal level. The DBS Bank also built a new Chatbot to assess candidates and answer their frequently asked questions. This Chatbot enables applicants to learn key information about the company and markets the company more efficiently to a wider audience. The company will, therefore, receive more applications from a wider pool of applicants and also have the capacity to deal with all the paperwork, which could easily overwhelm a small team of people (Meister, 2019).

Human Skills That Cannot Be Automated Will Become More Important

In the coming age, the skills that make us unique as humans will continue to be important. With the creation of millions of new jobs that are related to artificial intelligence, digital literacy will become paramount for individuals. But what is absolutely needed are the skills that are social and human, including empathy. For example, Bank of America is leading a national training program that is going to teach empathy to customer service workers in banks (Meister, 2019). One of the ways they do this is by putting their associates in situations where they must use their empathetic skills to identify with their customers. This includes whenever a customer gets easily frustrated or upset while talking on the phone because of some kind of situation. One example is using an online tool or app for the phone. A person could call customer service and get support about that tool. However, the customer could suddenly become upset over the usage of the tool and will want to speak to someone about it over the phone. The customer service associate must then be aware of the emotions of their customers to provide the best support.

Empathy is especially important for people who are working in the service industry. It is a human trait that cannot be replicated by a machine. Also, emotional intelligence is a key factor in contributing to better job performance for workers (Meister, 2019).

AI is not going to take away jobs but Rather Help Workers Do Their Jobs Better

AI is going to create more jobs than it eliminates. For HR leaders, this means that they will have to look at the process of recruiting new talent and re-imagine the candidate experience.

Case Study #2

Hilton is using AI in the process of HR recruitment. By using AI, they can screen and interview candidates with an increased speed of 85%. This has enabled the company to receive more applications and more diverse candidates, which can help HR specialists to identify the best candidates for the job. Having started to use AI in 2014, Hilton will continue to use technology to help them streamline the hiring process to make it simpler for people to sift through mountains of applications of those applying to become an employee at the Hilton Company (Meister, 2019).

New Jobs Will Be Created Using Artificial Intelligence.

Creating new jobs is going to be a thing of the future, which will be a top priority for people in 2019. Below are some examples.

Voice UX Designer

This job will use the voice as a platform to deliver a dialect and sound that is pleasing to everyone. The Voice UX Designer will create AI tools and algorithms to help people find their voice assistant (Meister, 2019).

Head of Business Behavior

This person will be in charge of analyzing employee's behavior, including information about how they are performing. Using the data that is generated from AI, the person can figure out how to challenge and work with the employees involved (Meister, 2019).

AI Trainer

This person will have the responsibility of preparing others to use AI effectively in the workplace (Meister, 2019).

An AI-Ready Workforce is a Key to a Better Future

As we are well into the middle of 2019, learning how to work with AI becomes increasingly important for us. By developing the workforce and training HR specialists, we can implement new strategies to help with recruiting and corporate learning. We can also identify new jobs and skills that are created by using AI.

Workers are looking for more than just money: Meaning

More and more workers are looking for work that brings meaning to their lives, not just a paycheck. A report from Meaning and Purpose at Work found that some workers would be willing to forego 23% of their entire future lifetime earnings to have a job that provided meaningful benefits to them (Meister, 2019). This means that having a meaningful life is more important than productivity for some employees. Furthermore, it points to the importance of being happy at work. Employees who find their work meaningful are less likely to quit their jobs and are more likely to stay at their work for longer. With more workers searching for meaning, HR specialists can play into that by promoting a culture that emphasizes meaning and purpose in a company's workspace.

Conclusion

With a more empathetic and caring workforce, we will find the need to train HR professionals to be at the top of their game. Although there are many problems that HR specialists must deal with every day, having AI helps them deal with the challenges that inevitably befall them. By giving them the ability to sift through large amounts of candidate data, they can spend more time on what's important, which is finding the right person for the job. Only when they can spend this time with the right people can they bring in new talent that will contribute to their company. It takes time, energy, and monetary resources to make this happen. But when it does, the company can find ways of increasing its presence in the world of business. That only happens by having a strong and stable workforce. Too many companies see the ebb and flow of time and experience shifts in new workers arriving and others leaving. It happens all the time, especially with millennials, who tend to move around a lot. What's important for the livelihood of a company is for leaders to find talent that can stick around for a long time. Companies need to invest a lot in the talent of their company and find the human resources that will bring value to the company. Using AI-ready individuals will make this possible. AI will propel all workers into a future of efficiency, empathy, and excellence. That's a future worth living and working for.

Chapter : 15
Business Intelligence and Analytics

"Data is what you need to do analytics. Information is what you need to do business."

– John Owen (Dufrene, 2017)

This chapter will discuss business intelligence (BI) and its relationship to AI, as well as business analytics. Finally, it will include three case studies of how this information is applied to the business sector.

In today's world, businesses are driven almost entirely by data. By now, AI is used to being used as a key component of everyday business practices, and Business Intelligence is playing a key role as well (Oswald, 2018).

Because there have been many advances in cognitive computing and AI, companies can now use algorithms to gain an understanding of consumer preferences, behaviors, among other things. They can use this information to produce insights that identify trends and make good decisions about how to improve their standing as a competitor in the market.

With many data sources continually developing, such as smartphones, tablets, and the Internet, businesses don't have to use large chunks of statistics from reports generated by business intelligence software. Instead, they can use more actionable insights (Oswal, 2018).

Now, businesses can develop analytics that gives real-time insights. These analytics make use of data while it's new and actionable.

Business Intelligence software is applicable in three different areas.

1. Descriptive analytics-- This is one of the simpler analytics. In this business intelligence system, the software summarizes data and tells the user what happened. It is descriptive. The analytics software will summarize raw data and break it down so it can easily be interpreted by a human. Descriptive analytics helps companies understand past trends and behaviors while learning what to do in the future (Oswal, 2018).
2. Predictive analytics-- This type of software "predicts" the future. This type of analytics provides companies with insights about their future. Although no predictive analytics software is perfect, organizations are increasingly relying on these analytics to predict future events for their company. This system uses probability to forecast the events within a company (Oswal, 2018).
3. Prescriptive analytics-- This type of analytics uses software to give advice about situations. These AI-powered analytics enable the user to predict what event will happen but also why it will happen (Oswal, 2018).

With the amazing progress of analytics and BI, businesses need to develop their decision-making skills. Business digitization is helping people gain prescriptive analytics to help grow their business.

How is AI Changing the Landscape of Businesses?

It's already making a big difference in industries, such as healthcare, financial services, science, and trade. For example, in medicine, AI is helping doctors to make faster and more accurate diagnoses. Additionally, it is helping to develop new prescription drugs (Oswall, 2018).

AI Influences Decision-Making

AI is making an impact on different parts of businesses today. It uses big data and then chews it up and breaks it down into insights that help CEOs and other managers to make decisions for their company. For example, a market manager must understand the customer's desires and needs to create products that align with those needs. AI helps to predict customer behavior and how to work with those forecasts.

AI insights are more reliable than before. AI offers real-time feedback, which helps to add to prescriptive models. This allows the prescribed advice to be better than any previous advice. The insights allow businesses to make better decisions based on automated decisions (Oswal, 2018).

Why Do Businesses Need to Have AI-Powered BI Systems?

AI-Powered BI Systems can allow businesses to have data transformed into simple, accurate reports and other documents. Why is this important?

1   Dashboards are not sufficient. Businesses need to have AI-powered BI tools, which help them to process all data and make reports that give quality insights on the data.
2   Get rid of large data overload. With data increasing in quantity, businesses are in need of tools to manage the load. Using business intelligence software will help

companies to break down the data into manageable parts that can be easily interpreted.

3   Get insights in real-time. Thanks to the fast-speed technology, businesses can make decisions swiftly and efficiently, because they can interpret the data right away and receive insights that enable them to do all the things they need to do to operate well (Oswal, 2018).

4   There are not enough data experts. According to a study from McKinsey, there are not enough data analytics professionals in the United States. Furthermore, there are only about 1.5 million analysts who can effectively interpret and use data (Oswall, 2018). It is important to have experienced users in data analytics in your team; however, it can be costly to do this. Making good decisions for your business in a timely manner requires having the right software.

This section will highlight several case studies on business intelligence apps, which are built for machine learning.

Case Study #1: HANA

HANA is SAP's (German multinational software company) cloud platform, which is used to manage large databases full of information. The app replicates and takes in data, which includes sales information and customer transactions, from different databases and sources.

This platform can be installed at the company through a cloud service. HANA will collect information from different devices, including phones, desktop PCs, among other points. If sales associates from your company use a smartphone or tablet, the customer transactions can be recorded to be analyzed and interpreted by HANA to give fresh insights to you.

Walmart has been using HANA to interpret the sales transaction records from its 11,000 stores within just a few seconds (Oswal, 2018).

How does Walmart use HANA?

There can be many fluctuations in business activity. For example, there might be too many product orders, or there may be slowdowns at a factory. Machine learning can determine what is going on with these discrepancies. For example, if a factory manager has the app on their PC, which monitors equipment on an assembly line, HANA can collect and process data from the slowdown. The results can then be analyzed.

Case Study #2: DOMO

DOMO is a business-management software tool, which creates a virtual dashboard on which companies can make business decisions. It uses cloud-based software and can be used with different sized companies from 20 to 500 employees. DOMO can use data from different sources, including Salesforce, Square, Facebook, and other apps to create insights on customer activity and interests.

In March 2019, DOMO announced the release of Mr. Roboto, which is an advice-giving tool that uses predictive and prescriptive analytics. This tool will facilitate better business decisions, including predicting the return on investment and sales decisions (Oswal, 2018).

Case Study #3: Avanade

Avanade is a software used by Microsoft and Accenture, which uses predictive analysis. It is used to give staff more perspective and insight on how to run a business. The goal is to use consumer data to help the team grow and develop. It helps the company to develop new products that are attractive to consumers.

The software has shown that the world is moving in the direction of using smart technologies to complete work that has only been done by humans and which can generate more revenue for businesses (Oswal, 2018).

Conclusion

It is important to note that analytics enables businesses to thrive and to develop their business strategy by closely monitoring data related to consumer transactions and other factors that influence decisions. It is vital that businesses use predictive and prescriptive analytics to produce good results that will help grow revenue and generate new sales. Then, businesses can easily target different groups of consumers and create products that enhance the company's image and standing in the economy.

Chapter : 16
Software Development

Some people call this artificial intelligence, but the reality is this technology will enhance us. So instead of artificial intelligence, I think we'll augment our intelligence."

— Ginni Rometty (Jacquet, 2019)

This chapter will explore how AI will influence the future of software development.

It has been estimated that AI tools will be able to generate 2.9 trillion USD in business revenue and value by 2021. 80% of businesses are starting to invest in AI. With this continued growth and development for AI, software development is also improving. Shawn Drost, the co-founder of Hack Reactor, has said that AI is continuing to influence software development, but only in small doses. It hasn't actually impacted the workflow that much so far (Dsouza, 2018).

However, AI is going to change how organizations complete their business operations and how they make apps smarter and more efficient. Consequently, software development will be influenced by AI. AI is going to improve the planning, development, and testing of software, which will create better software in different business environments.

Software engineering contains five key components, including the following: software design, software testing, GUI testing, strategic decision making, and automated code-generation (Dsouza, 2018). These areas are ones that could benefit from AI. Automated testing and bug detection tools are currently areas of interest for applying AI to the software.

After that, we will see more AI in software design, business decision-making, and software deployment (Dsouza, 2018).

Software design

Developing software design requires advanced expertise and experience. The first thing a designer does is envision the solution to a problem and then investigate it thoroughly before reaching a solution.

AI development has demonstrated a benefit to software development. In one example, the Artificial Intelligence Design Assistant (AIDA), created by Bookmark, helps understand a user's needs and desires and uses this information to generate a website for the user. AIDA uses millions of combinations to create a customized user experience. Within two minutes, it can design the first draft of a website (Dsouza, 2018).

Software testing

Applications interact with one another and create complex problems for users every day. As they increase in complexity, they can be addressed by new machine-based technology. AI tools can test information, assess the authenticity of the information, and offer support for test management. AI can help ensure that testing is free of mistakes. With automated software tests, testers don't need to use manual tests anymore. This saves time, energy, and money.

Case Study #1

Functionalize is a tool that tests software fast and efficiently using AI cloud testing. Users must type a test plan in English, and then the information will become a test case. The tool can be used on every browser and device in the cloud. Another example of a tester is Sapfix, which fixes bugs called Sapienz. The tool then offers fixes for software engineers to use in their development of software (Dsouza, 2018).

GUI Testing

Graphic User Interfaces (GUI) are an important part of today's software development. They are used in critical systems and help avoid glitches through testing. With few AI tools to help, testing GUIs is a challenging and arduous process for software engineers (Dsouza, 2018).

At the moment, GUI testing methods can only be done by a software designer, who does many homogeneous tasks, including identifying conditions to check during testing and evaluating the GUI software. It's a lot of work for one person to do. GUI testers must also modify tests and change test suites. Testing today is intensive and can be difficult to do.

One AI tool that is transforming software development is Applitools, which is a GUI tester. It automatically tests if a visual code is working or not. Applitools allows its users to test their visual code to make sure the visual presentation of the app is the way it's intended to be. With multiple screen layouts, the app makes sure all the design options are shown the way they are intended to. Additionally, this app helps users to track web page activity and the look of the webpage being designed (Dsouza, 2018).

Applying AI to Decision-Making

Usually, developers have to go through an involved process to decide what needs to be featured in a product. Through machine learning, AI can help analyze the performance of existing apps on the market, which helps teams of software designers and project managers to find solutions to make a positive impact and reduce risks.

This process usually takes a very long time. But with machine learning helping with software development, companies can significantly cut the time required to process, deliver software products, and increase revenue.

AI Canvas is a popular tool used in strategic decision making (Dsouza, 2018). It helps to identify important questions and addresses the problems that arise with creating and using machine learning models for business.

AI Canvas is used when companies need to do seven things: redaction, judgment, action, outcome, input, training, and giving feedback (Dsouza, 2018). If the business can clearly execute these processes, then they can identify areas where AI can lower costs and improve performance.

Automatic Code Generation and Programming Assistants

An AI programming assistant can significantly decrease a programmer's workload of coding a big project.

Developers have tried to create systems that can code, but these methods cannot easily deal with details that must be interpreted effectively. Writing code involves human processing. However, there is one programming assistant called Bayou, which is intended to extract knowledge from online source code repositories, such as GitHub (Dsouza, 2018). It makes programming easier and error-free.

Conclusion

Software development has improved a lot over the past several years. AI and software development tools are making it simpler to create software. The Forrester Research report talks about how AI is helping software development with automated testing and other tools (Dsouza, 2018). With new technology, AI is expected to be faster, more efficient, and less expensive for businesses to use. It allows the software to be developed in a way that benefits everyone involved. Additionally, it makes the features more user-friendly and helpful.

Chapter : 17
Marketing

Artificial intelligence and machine learning, as a dominant discipline within AI, is an amazing tool. In and of itself, it's not good or bad. It's not a magic solution. It isn't the core of the problems in the world."

— Vivienne Ming, Executive Chair & Co-Founder, Socos Labs (Honjo, 2019)

Artificial intelligence is becoming a very important part of many industries, including business and marketing.

Let's look at some ways that AI can be used in the marketing industry.

Product recommendations

Way back in 1998, marketing experts began to predict consumer behavior using digital bookshelves, a concept developed by Jussi Karlgren, the Swedish computational linguist. In that year, Amazon started to filter results to create product recommendations for consumers (Sentance, 2019).

Now that we are in 2019, many of the most successful digital companies are presenting their products through personalized content recommendations. This includes companies like Spotify, Amazon, and Netflix. AI has been clustering and interpreting consumer data and has been adapting the marketing strategies to suit the desires and tastes of its consumers.

Many other brands are beginning to follow the fold with their own AI-designed recommendations for consumers. One example is Sky, which has a machine-learning device that recommends products for consumers based on their mood. Because consumers are accustomed to using personalized recommendations from Netflix and Amazon, they are also looking for customized options with other brands. Additionally, publishing companies are offering their own AI-powered content recommendations to suit the needs of readers (Sentance, 2019).

Data Analysis and Filtering

These days, marketing has continued to develop based on data-driven results. Interpreting and using data for the purpose of developing business strategies has helped enhance customer experience and targeting.

Putting together all of this data can be time-consuming and difficult for humans to perform. Also, there is room for human error, which can be eliminated by using machines. AI enters the picture and provides data analysis, which would be difficult or impossible for humans to perform and gives humans the ability to carry out more intuitive, complex, and creative work (Sentance, 2019).

Case Study #1

AI is being used to improve account marketing. One personalization company is called Demandbase, which uses AI to filter out companies from prospects that would make a company lose revenue over a long period (Sentance, 2019).

Demandbase is a statistics-based company that wants to find ways to avoid companies that could lose them money. AI can help them identify "timely intent" while showing accounts where there is an increased opportunity of selling a product before a competitor is made (Sentance, 2019).

Search Engines

AI has facilitated greater searches online. In 2015, Google started to use AI in its searches by employing RankBrain, a machine-learning-based algorithm. After that, many eCommerce websites followed the fold and used AI in their search engines to make product searches more fun, interactive, and sophisticated (Sentance, 2019).

Using natural language processing, search engines can figure out what the links are between products and suggested items for consumers, helping consumers to find products that they may not even be looking for.

Visual recognition

AI image search and analysis is helping people find things using graphics. Image search is something that helps users find graphics that are similar to each other in the same way that text is used. Image search includes technology like Google Lens.

Image search can help with marketing apps and retaining information. It can help improve and personalize a customer's shopping experience. Using images, customers can determine if they want to buy a recommended product.

Case Study #2

Target is partnering with Asos' Style Match, which is a method of searching that allows shoppers to take a picture of the product and upload it to the tool while searching the catalog for similar items. This tool encourages the shopper to search through the webpage and then go to the store to buy the product. It helps the shopper find the ideal purchase even if they have no idea what they are searching for (Sentance, 2019.)

Image recognition helps marketers find uses for brand logos and products, and to spot trends. This method is known as "visual social listening" (Sentance, 2019).

Social Listening and Feelings Analysis

Natural language processing is becoming very useful for marketers who want to understand their brand's presence and bring people into the conversation about the brand through advertising.

Nowadays, AI permits brands to analyze the feelings of their customers and understand issues and problems with their products. Samsung detected customer dissatisfaction on its S8 smartphone due to a red tint display on the screen. They discovered this through "listening" to social media and to people who were voicing their disappointment (Sentance, 2019).

Marketers can use social media to find out what consumers are saying about their products. However, marketers need to be very careful with how they approach this type of marketing because of the risk of scaring people.

Product Pricing

With AI, products can be priced with greater optimization and accuracy, because the devices can take a lot of data into consideration. Machine learning can also be used for dynamic pricing, which looks at customer data and patterns to predict what customers are willing to pay, as well as their desire to take on offers. This allows businesses to be more precise with their targeting and provide discounts to sell a product.

One brand that is using dynamic pricing is Airbnb, which helps property owners provide the right price based on the location, property features, local events, photos, reviews, and other factors (Sentance, 2019).

Audience Targeting

The next feature of AI marketing is audience targeting, which enables marketers to reach their audience with greater personalization. Using the data that they collect, marketers can segment their customers and analyze past behaviors (Sentance, 2019). An example of this is when the AI can analyze how a buyer will act after purchasing something on the Internet and use predictive analytics to forecast what they will buy next.

Chatbots and Conversational AI

Chatbots have been an increasingly important presence in AI in recent years. Singapore uses Bus Uncle chat, which gathers information on public transport ETA and answers questions via Facebook Messenger. Other brands are starting to develop conversational voice experiences that will help customers with their shopping experiences. Trainline, which is a UK transportation reservation system, recently developed a voice app for Google Assistant. With the help of this machine learning feature, the lives of commuters in the UK have been enhanced (Sentance, 2019).

Voice Recognition

Voice recognition systems have been continually updated over the years to meet customer demands. Google has wanted to develop voice recognition technology so that it can have 99% accuracy. Currently, Baidu has claimed to have reached an accuracy rate of 97% (Sentance, 2019).

Conclusion

AI is going to reinvent the way we work, shop, the market completely, and sell, and it will allow us to do things that we never thought we could. However, AI is only going to be the best it can be if the people who are operating it make it that way. AI and machine learning still require human manipulation to improve its accuracy and algorithms.

Eventually, AI could transform the economy by creating new products, business models, and envisioning future possibilities that were not seen before. But that could take a long time to develop. Everyone needs to stay on the same page of understanding both the limits and capabilities of AI so that new developments and improvements can be made in marketing technology.

Chapter : 18
Sales

This chapter will explore the role of artificial intelligence in the sales of products and services of companies.

Companies are starting to use AI in creative ways to make their business grow. If you've ever browsed through Netflix to find a film to watch, AI would have influenced your decision about what you will end up watching. If you've ever used Uber to get a ride, AI would have been used to track down a car and find one in your immediate vicinity. If you've been thinking about buying a product or going on a vacation, AI undoubtedly would have been analyzing your online activity (Antonio, 2018).

Such algorithms facilitate an organization's decision-making process to forecast improved predictions. Based on research from the book Sales Ex Machina: How Artificial Intelligence is Changing the World of Selling, there are five areas where AI can help businesses grow by increasing sales (Antonio, 2018).

Price Optimization

Giving a discount is a sales strategy used by many people in sales. It is not always easy knowing what kind of discount should be given to a customer. However, now an AI algorithm can tell you what a good discount would be to guarantee that you can nail the deal by looking at what aspects made a successful deal in the past. Such aspects could include the price, product specification compliance, number of competitors, company size, among many other factors (Antonio, 2018).

Sales Forecasts

Managers have to determine how many sales will be made each quarter. Now, they can use an AI algorithm, which enables them to predict the next quarter's revenue, which would help them to generate a better inventory of resources. Knowing how and when sales will happen is helpful to sales managers so they can target the right people. If they know how much revenue needs to be coming in, then they can make an effort to get the right work done to generate more sales. The only way they can know this is by using AI technology, which makes everything easier for them (Antonio, 2018).

Upselling and Cross-Selling

The best way to get more revenue is by targeting current clients. But you have to determine who will buy more. You can spend a lot on marketing to customers, who will not buy, or you can try to identify which of your current customers will be more likely to buy an enhanced version of what they have, or which ones would like to buy a brand-new product. The result of this effort is an increase in the overall revenue, as well as a drop in the marketing costs (Antonio, 2018).

Lead Scoring

Salespeople have to make decisions on which clients to target every day. Determining where to focus their time and energy is always difficult. Many times, decisions are made based on a person's intuition or incomplete information. However, if AI is considered, then algorithms can use customer activity and social media to find opportunities and leads that seal the deal and bring in new sales (Antonio, 2018).

Performance Management

Each month, managers must think about revenue sources and find out which salespeople are likely to reach their targets, as well as which deals are most likely to be made. With AI, sales managers can determine which salespeople can seal the best deals, which helps their business meet their quotas.

Where is the Best Place to Begin Using AI in Sales?

If you want to use AI in your sales department, you need first to acquire data that can help you understand your client base. For example, the sales department has to have a history of purchase data and analytics from promotions. Using this data, AI can make predictions about who will be a possible buyer. Next, the data sets need to include Customer Relationship Management platforms (CRM), including Microsoft 365, Salesforce.com, among others. Using these platforms will help you to analyze data sets and understand the various patterns and predictions (Antonio, 2018).

Case Study

CRM companies are adding AI options to their platforms. Salesforce.com has AppExchange, where consumers can buy AI plug-ins to record, store, and analyze phone calls (Antonio, 2018). This information can then be directly interpreted for marketing experts to find out which consumers would possibly buy different products. This seems to be a bit like 1984 in which Big Brother is watching out for everyone. Unfortunately, it can be a bit difficult to cope with how sales companies can watch our every move. But this is the future of sales, and it is enabling companies to grow their business in new and innovative ways.

Conclusion

Sales are being increasingly influenced by the development of AI technology. What makes it both fascinating and disturbing is the fact that people are monitored more closely than ever before, and thus, their activities are no longer private but rather part of the data collection process. With more data available to sales associates and managers, they have more power to leverage over customers and how they can nail the next deal because they know what the customer needs and wants. They can plan accordingly by targeting the right customers that they can make a deal with, analyze past spending patterns, and understand how customers will react to future situations. What's clear is that AI is going to transform the world of sales so that companies will be able to generate a lot more income. Each company has a lot to gain by investing in new AI technology, which will enhance their sales strategies and customer base.

Chapter : 19
Customer Support

"The future of personalized customer experience is inevitably tied to 'Intelligent Assistance.'"

–Dan Miller, Founder, Opus Research | Medium (Sowards, 2016)

This chapter will highlight what AI can bring to improved customer support.

What keeps a customer coming back to a product or service? It is the quality of the customer service at hand. Many companies have been investing in CRM technology because of its blend of "intelligence" and "automation." This customer service becomes uniquely powered by AI (Sharma, 2018).

From ordering into making appointments with doctors and hair stylists, customers are enjoying the benefits of automation, and so are businesses. Experts are predicting that approximately 85% of customer service requests may be handled by AI as soon as 2020. How exactly could AI transform customer service and reinvent it (Sharma, 2018)?

Problem Solving for the Future

People who are not happy with their customer experience won't buy the product being marketed. But with AI intelligence agents, data can be processed and analyzed from previous interactions. Then, the agents can produce relevant offers, which can attract customers and reduce their frustration and departures. With interactive problem-solving,

AI provides solutions to the problems of abandonment of purchase and helps customer satisfaction to improve drastically.

With AI, There Can Be Reduced Cost for Hiring Customer Service Agents

Customer service is a sector with a lot of turnovers. This is an unfortunate reality for many companies. When a company hires a customer service agent, they have to invest anywhere from $3,000 to $4,000 USD. Add training to that package, and then you're looking at $4,500 USD (Sharma, 2018). However, that is not the issue at stake. What a challenge is having to incur this expense over and over due to high turnover rates?

Therefore, the solution that will help companies in AI. One example of this solution is IBM Watson. This AI tool is responsible for helping IBM with millions of customer service transactions, which can be reconfigured for many different cases.

Customer Service 24/7/365 without the extra expenses

Many companies operate with a workforce that is in different locations and time zones. Therefore, customer service can be a very expensive ordeal for them. This is where AI comes to the rescue. It helps collect a vast amount of information within the company to answer repetitive questions. Then, the software can be used to answer customer service questions using email, chatbots, and phone support but without the need of a human at the wheel. If a business uses this AI, then the possibility for profit and gain is significant.

AI-influenced Customer Service Centers

AI will continue to be influenced by human customer service agents. But having AI-influenced customer service centers can be a great resource for the future, as AI and natural language processing technology collaborates to monitor daily customer transactions. The use of AI will then provide important recommendations to customer service agents as to how to respond to and deal with customer inquiries and problems (Sharma, 2018).

With this application, time to resolve the situation will be greatly reduced, and customer service agents won't have to develop a lot of knowledge about products and services, which makes it easy for businesses to train and develop new talent in the customer service team as turnover happens.

The Use of Chatbots

With the introduction of chatbots, customer service has been more customized and automated using instant messaging services and natural language processing. These bots can answer customer concerns 24/7 through the instant messaging service, which can begin and continue the conversation. Many organizations are using chatbots for their customer service, including banks, grocery stores, and retail stores. Personalized conversations with these bots will help develop revenue sources for companies (Sharma, 2018).

Instantaneous support helps customer satisfaction

With little room for error or delays in typing, customer service using bots is the way of the future. AI-powered self-service portals help provide an exchange of information in close to real-time. Inquiries and concerns are resolved a lot more quickly and efficiently, which leads to greater customer satisfaction. AI tools can quickly find information through scanning databases and can show it on the screen or in other ways.

Is AI the Cure-All?

AI devices can only work if they are commanded by human agents. They can understand customer intentions and reactions using the responses generated by a human being. Therefore, companies need to continually train and develop their AI devices to adapt to their business strategies.

To achieve full-AI capacity, companies should start by building data warehouses, processes, and other tools, which will help AI devices to learn fast and effectively. In addition, workflows must allow for inquiries and complaints to come to human customer service agents prior to being outsourced to robots. The important thing is training devices to perform with a complementary effort to human service agents (Sharma, 2018).

Case Study #1

One company is using AI-augmented messaging, LivePerson, which has a revenue of $200 million (Walker, 2019). It is currently working in tandem with IBM Watson. The company is using a model that provides a collaboration between bot and agent. Instead of providing a service that is purely automated, the service provides a unique option of partial automation in which the robot provides some support. But, when the inquiry becomes too complex for a machine to handle, the human intervenes and finishes the job before handing off the job to a bot for a simpler reply. This exchange between bot and human provides greater reliability for the use of the service. LivePerson has claimed that about half of all customer service interactions can use robots. With this new system, one agent can handle multiple customer interactions at once. For example, customer service agents at UPC, one of Ireland's Internet service providers, can process three chats at once (Walker, 2019).

Case Study #2

Having people read all emails a company receives and understanding how to resolve customer complaints, inquiries, and other issues can be a very challenging and time-consuming task. Furthermore, many companies are using AI to help make the process move faster and more efficiently.

One company is using the tool, DigitalGenius as their customer service product. Some companies use this AI technology tool to label emails to route them to the correct department. Magoosh, the student test prep company, has been using DigitalGenius to make its customer service team operate more efficiently. Thanks to DigitalGenius, Magoosh cut down the customer waiting time by 50% and enabled Magoosh to reach their daily goal of replying to customer requests within 24 hours (Walker, 2019).

Conclusion

AI is making an impact on customer service and its evolution. It is being used to improve and cut down on the costs of customer service in a variety of fields, including the food industry, retail, and insurance. Companies recognize that AI chatbots and voice recognition systems can handle low-level requests that are typical everyday interactions with customer service agents.

Although AI is making important changes, it is important to note that it will never fully replace human agents. However, AI can take a bit of the monotony of everyday interactions that can be taxing on humans and create a turnover rate in the customer service industry. This means that there will be cheaper and more effective services offered. But investment must be continually made to enhance the services for people to enjoy better customer service. This is the way of the future.

Chapter : 20
The Ethics of Enterprise AI

"At Microsoft, our goal is that AI systems amplify human ingenuity. Ethical decision-making frameworks help ensure we are building AI systems based on a set of shared values and principles, and we are excited that companies like integrate.ai are helping drive clarity for business leaders as they consider development and deployment of AI systems."

— Andree Gagnon, Assistant General Counsel, Microsoft Canada ("The Ethics of Artificial Intelligence," n.d.)

Ethics of Artificial Intelligence

Artificial intelligence is among the biggest and most potentially "disruptive" influences in the technology of our modern era. Understanding the underlying ethical concerns could be one of the most crucial issues to be considered by human beings ("The Ethics of Artificial Intelligence," n.d.).

Understanding the ethics of artificial intelligence and knowing how to develop ethical machine learning systems will be a crucial part of every business strategy going forward. Although artificial intelligence has the capacity to do great things for your business, if you don't have an ethical strategy to approach it, your company could suffer devastating consequences.

Best case scenario, you could put your business at serious risk. But at its worst point, you could severely impact the entire society. Artificial intelligence can change how businesses develop their ties with their clients. When a business uses data and machine learning, they can find out what people want and value in their lives. In addition, they can lead to big sales closures and deal with people by directly relating to customers who are guaranteed to contribute a lot to the business ("The Ethics of Artificial Intelligence," n.d.).

On the flip side of that, businesses must use data from AI in unique ways. Businesses must respect the data of customers and use it wisely. You have to maintain the trust of the customer. Otherwise, you could severely damage the relationship through leaks of private information or by directly manipulating customer behavior. Trust is something that you develop over the years with someone. It is something that can be either gained or lost in an instant.

Furthermore, it is necessary that people utilize a risk-based approach to the ethical use of AI because data is very sensitive ("The Ethics of Artificial Intelligence," n.d.). Businesses must think about the potential risks of using customer data to perform various functions for the business. By erring on the side of caution, the business can operate in a wise and effective way. Ultimately, everyone needs to be on the same page when it comes to the values and focus of ethical AI systems.

Principles for Ethical AI in Your Business

To help your organization adopt a responsible and ethical AI, there are several principles and questions that your company needs to think about ("The Ethics of Artificial Intelligence," n.d.).

1   If you want the future to differ from the past, so that you don't perpetuate any biases, you need to take this

into account when designing a machine learning system.

2 Clarify what proxy metrics you are going to use and don't optimize anything. Doing so will make bias worse and lead to consequences that compromise your values.

3 When dealing with abstractions and groupings, there is always a risk of unethical treatment of people.

4 Know the sensitive data sources and handle them ethically and carefully.

5 It is important to have the right context for explaining the technology. In addition, it is important to maintain transparency in every aspect of doing business so that there is no undercover action occurring.

6 Privacy concerns are always an issue for customers. Therefore, creating a safe environment for the diffusion of information needs to conform to social norms and rules.

7 Troubleshooting any concerns is also a key part of managing errors and mistakes that happen along the way after machine learning models are implemented.

8 Be in touch with the community and customers to hear their concerns about privacy and ethics.

AI promises to be an amazing contribution to our society and businesses. With our increased ability to process the data on a massive scale, relationships between consumers and the businesses have changed. Because of machine learning models, customers are driving interactions with companies by providing feedback on what they want and value in society. Like in personal relationships, businesses can use this feedback to manufacture products and offer services that consumers want. If we want AI to have a positive impact on our society, we have to develop a mindset in which we imagine what it can do for us and the things we can use it.

To move forward in the future, we need to integrate innovative approaches to machine learning. AI will be a growing presence in our lives in the future. While it has great potential to improve our lives, it can also have a negative impact on us. To avoid this, it's important that we ask questions that can allow us to express our key values that will help with the research and development of AI.

Case Study: Rachel at IBM

Rachel worked for IBM computers and was in charge of the data collection and analysis of sensitive information for consumers, including credit card data and other transactions that were used and secured by the company. Recognizing that AI was handling a lot of this sensitive data, Rachel was concerned about the privacy of the information involved, and therefore she worked hard to secure the data and made sure that it was encrypted and destroyed in some cases. Rachel worked tirelessly to help secure the data of millions of customers for this corporation. When she had an interview with a local news firm, she talked about the importance of safety and security in the digital age. Here are some of her remarks.

Rachel: I believe we currently live and work in one of the most advanced and yet dangerous eras of our time. With technology moving faster than the speed of light in a figurative sense, we are experiencing new growth in technology at increased rates. The thing is, with more power, comes more responsibility. We need to take responsibility for the advances in technology by handling sensitive information with care. We cannot simply allow AI devices to handle all the sensitive data that we have in our systems. We should have AI trainers, who are going to manage the devices to support and secure consumer and business information. Then, we should put a lid on the security settings on all the features of our apps and devices. By raising security concerns, we can find ways to keep our future safe. There is always a danger of putting technology in the wrong hands. Malicious predators exist out there to search and destroy corporations and individuals. We must be vigilant to handle all the future issues of privacy and security. We cannot be complacent or unwilling to move forward. Instead, we must work to advance technology in ways that will benefit everyone in the world and keep people safe from harm's way. That is the concern of ethical AI and should be at the top of everyone's priority list.

Conclusion

Ethics is at the heart of effective AI. It is the only way that we can go forward with our sales and marketing strategies. Too much is at stake if we choose to forgo the safety and security of our data sources. We must be vigilant in keeping our customers safe in the midst of a difficult world. While AI technology is something that people are increasingly relying upon, it is not fool-proof and can fail us. We must be mindful of the limits of technology and how it can lead to devastating situations if we are not careful. We live in a dark world. People will take advantage of the limited security features that we have. No one can be too safe or cautious at this time. Therefore, we should be very careful to make ethical concerns a part of our plans and how we can create a more sustainable future with AI.

Summary and Additional Resources

"Artificial intelligence will reach human levels by around 2029. Follow that out further to, say, 2045, and we will have multiplied the intelligence, the human biological machine intelligence of our civilization a billion-fold." – Ray Kurzweil (Brown, 2019)

The world is not what it was a few decades ago. We're constantly moving forward at seemingly lightning speed. Technology continues to advance every year, which has led to advancements in how our workplace is run to how we spend time online doing shopping. And increasingly, we are seeing that artificial intelligence is becoming a more prevalent presence in our lives. Whether we like or not, artificial intelligence (AI) is on the horizon to transform our world.

To prepare for this profound change, we must equip our businesses and workplaces. Get ready for transformation beyond your wildest imagination. AI is going to help our workforce get off its feet and do amazing things in the world. With AI technology, businesses will operate more efficiently than ever before. More people will want to work for companies who use AI because they provide a great working environment that encourages growth, collaboration, and creativity. Using AI is going to increase our capacities beyond what they used to be. In the past, we may not have been able to do as much work. Thanks to AI, we will be able to more than double or triple our workload now and have more time to do the things that need to get done. Gone are the days that we thought we didn't have enough time to do things that we wanted to do. Now, we have AI to help us navigate through all the challenges of the 21st century.

Thank you for choosing this book for your exploration of artificial intelligence. We hope that you have enjoyed exploring the topic in depth using a variety of case studies, examples, and illustrations that bring you into the world of artificial intelligence. Throughout this book, we have talked about how AI is impacting the global workplace and its contributions to business and marketing. Admittedly, it is a large topic that is continually being investigated and examined today. We tried to provide the most relevant and updated information from the past year or two, which provides you with the resources that are necessary to understand the topic. But there is still much more to learn. In addition to the readings, it would be great to take an online course on artificial intelligence or some other form of training that would go more in-depth. MIT's OpenCourseWare provides a wide variety of lectures, readings, and other resources to help you learn more. Likewise, you can also take a course on artificial intelligence from the MIT Sloan School.

Here is a list of the best resources that you can consult about AI, that will help you in your research and learning:

Resources

1   This resource comes from Google, and it helps you to understand what machine learning is. You can complete this course in about one hour. https://developers.google.com/machine-learning/problem-framing/
2   Artificial Intelligence: Principles and Techniques from Stanford University
3   http://web.stanford.edu/class/cs221/

4   CS405: Artificial Intelligence. This is another online course that can be completed independently. https://learn.saylor.org/course/view.php?id=96
5   CS188: Intro to Artificial Intelligence, UC Berkeley. This online courseware is provided by one of the top universities in the nation. http://ai.berkeley.edu/lecture_videos.html
6   EdX: This free course is provided by Columbia University. You can take it for free, but if you want to be certified, you can pay $300 for certification. https://www.edx.org/course/artificial-intelligence-ai-columbiax-csmm-101x-0
7   Artificial Intelligence A to Z: Learn How to Build an AI at Udemy. https://www.udemy.com/artificial-intelligence-az/. This used to be $200, but it's now only $12.
8   Artificial Intelligence: A Modern Approach by Stuart Russell and Peter Norvig. Find it on Amazon: https://www.amazon.com/gp/product/0137903952
9   Foundations of Statistical Natural Language Processing by Christopher Manning. Find it at Amazon: https://www.amazon.com/gp/product/026213
10 Grokking Deep Learning in the Motion video course, which takes you on a journey of discovery about deep learning techniques to use: https://www.manning.com/livevideo/grokking-deep-learning-in-motion

Challenges in the Future but the Promise of Development

The road to using AI in our everyday lives is a long one. There will always be resistance from different people to use it, because of the effects that it could have on the volition of humanity and the compromise of human values. AI is still a taboo topic, especially among people from the older generation. However, AI has many promising aspects, which should soothe the fears and challenges of every person. AI is not going to be the end of humanity, but rather the beginning of something that can profoundly change our lives. We are standing on the brink of an amazing future. Things are only going to get better because the progress of human achievement is making AI into something that will be completely indispensable to us.

What's more, AI is going to be more essential to the operation of our businesses. We will not be able to do without AI in the coming days, because it is going to steer our businesses in the right direction. It cannot do so without the continued guidance and leading qualities of human beings, who will advocate for the use of machine learning technology. There will always be a necessary oversight to help the machines to operate at their best. We should stop seeing AI as a hindrance or danger to our systems and rather, see the window of opportunity that it presents to us, as it directs us to a prosperous period in our projected earnings, as well as customers, who will come to our companies. Let us promote the use and development of AI for a better future.

Businesses will continually need to update their knowledge of artificial intelligence, as it is always changing. With the future of superhuman intelligence in robots approaching, we will see more robots doing human-like things. We should never fear the takeover of robots in the world. Robots never think only about their own existence. Instead, they think of all the ways that they can live up to the objective that is provided by their human masters. That is why artificial intelligence will always be a human-controlled phenomenon that will develop until the end of time. It is a very exciting time to be living where robots will yield more influence over our lives increasingly.

Robots will continue to shape our future and lead us to paths where we never thought we could go. Let us watch as robots prepare us to take on the unknown and face our fears in ways that we never could before. Be prepared to be challenged and amazed. Let us aspire to move forward with one profound step into a future of innovation, efficiency, profitability, and empathy. That's the world in which we ought to live this year, 2019.

Bibliography

Adams, R.L. (2017). 10 Powerful Examples of Artificial Intelligence in Use Today. Forbes Magazine Online. Retrieved from

https://www.forbes.com/sites/robertadams/2017/01/10/1 0-powerful-examples-of-artificial-intelligence-in-use-today/#265c7a87420d

Antonio, V. (2018). How AI is Changing Sales. Harvard Business Review. https://hbr.org/2018/07/how-ai-is-changing-sales

Artificial Intelligence Quotes (n.d.). Good Reads. Retrieved from https://www.goodreads.com/quotes/tag/artificial-intelligence

Brown, A. (2019). 11 Quotes about AI That'll Make You Think. Technopedia. Retrieved from https://www.techopedia.com/11-quotes-about-ai-thatll-make-you-think/2/33718

Chan, B.K. (n.d.). Collect Data Properly for AI Machine Learning. Medium. Retrieved from https://medium.com/taming-artificial-intelligence/collect-data-properly-for-ai-machine-learning-dfb22da0cbf7

Davey, L. (n.d.) Humans vs. Robots: The Difference between AI and AGI. Medium. Retrieved from

https://becominghuman.ai/humans-vs-robots-the-difference-between-ai-and-agi-95197e1db279

Dsouza, M. (2018). 5 Ways Artificial Intelligence Is Upgrading Software. Packt. Retrieved from https://hub.packtpub.com/5-ways-artificial-intelligence-is-upgrading-software-engineering/

DuFrene, C. (2017). Top 5 Quotes About Data Quotes from 2016. Pyramid Analytics. Retrieved from https://www.pyramidanalytics.com/blog/details/our-top-5-data-quotes-from-2016

Groopman,J. (2018). How Investing in AI is About Investing in People, Not JustTechnology. Entrepreneur Asia Pacific. Retrieved from https://www.entrepreneur.com/article/320422

Honjo, Kim (2019). 32 AI Quotes from the Experts.[blog] Salesforce Blog. Retrieved from https://www.salesforce.com/blog/2019/04/ai-quotes.html

Jacquet, F. (2019). 12 Quotes that Question AI in 2019. DZone. Retrieved from https://dzone.com/articles/12-quotes-to-question-artificial-intelligence-in-2

Khurana, S. (2017). How to Develop an AI-readyCulture in your organization. Medium Corporation. Retrieved from https://medium.com/@subinder/https-medium-com-subinder-how-to-develop-an-ai-ready-culture-in-your-organization-11008b90ce11

Kolbjornsrud, V., Amico, R., and Thomas, R.(2016). How Artificial Intelligence Will Redefine Management. Harvard Business Review. Retrieved from https://hbr.org/2016/11/how-artificial-intelligence-will-redefine-management

Lath, A. (2018). 6 Challenges of Artificial Intelligence. BBN Times. Retrieved from https://www.bbntimes.com/en/companies/6-challenges-of-artificial-intelligence

Manyika, J. and Bughin, J. (2018). The Promise and Challenge of the Age of Artificial Intelligence. McKinsey and Company. Retrieved from https://www.mckinsey.com/featured-insights/artificial-intelligence/the-promise-and-challenge-of-the-age-of-artificial-intelligence

Mehta, P. (2018). Artificial Intelligence: Key Challenges and Opportunities. Forbes India. Retrieved from http://www.forbesindia.com/blog/technology/artificial-intelligence-key-challenges-and-opportunities/

Meister, J. (2019). Ten HR Trends in the Age of Artificial Intelligence. Forbes Magazine. Retrieved from https://www.forbes.com/sites/jeannemeister/2019/01/08/ten-hr-trends-in-the-age-of-artificial-intelligence/#9bd1f0f3219d

Morikawa, R. (2018). Best AI Experiments to Explore the Power of Machine Learning. Medium.com. Retrieved from https://medium.com/datadriveninvestor/the-best-ai-experiments-to-explore-the-power-of-machine-learning-eb2433c4b050

Nine Essentials for Enabling an AI-Ready Culture and Business (2019). Forbes Magazine. Retrieved from https://www.forbes.com/sites/insights-microsoftai/2019/02/04/nine-essentials-for-enabling-an-ai-ready-culture-and-business/#1d62e75d18c7

Novoseltseva, E. (2018). Artificial Intelligence in Ecommerce: Benefits, Statistics, Facts, Use Cases, and Case Studies.

Apiumhub. Retrieved from https://apiumhub.com/tech-blog-barcelona/artificial-intelligence-ecommerce/

Oswal, N. (2018). How AI Is Transforming Business Intelligence. Dataconomy.com. Retrieved from https://dataconomy.com/2018/02/ai-transforming-business-intelligence/

Roman, V. (2018). How to Develop a Machine

Learning Model from Scratch. Medium.com. Retrieved from https://towardsdatascience.com/machine-learning-general-process-8f1b510bd8af

Ross, A. (2018). Seven Steps to Successful AI Implementation with Prentiss Donohue.

Information-Age. Retrieved from https://www.information-age.com/successful-ai-implementation-123474050/

Rosso, C. (2018). 20 Great Quotes on Artificial

Intelligence. Psychology Today. Retrieved from https://www.psychologytoday.com/us/blog/the-future-brain/201805/20-great-quotes-artificial-intelligence

Ruth, J-P. (2019). 6 Examples of AI in Business Intelligence Applications. Emerj.com. Retrieved from https://emerj.com/ai-sector-overviews/ai-in-business-intelligence-applications/

Sentence, R. (2019). 15 Examples of Artificial

Intelligence in Marketing. Econsultancy. Retrieved from https://econsultancy.com/15-examples-of-artificial-intelligence-in-marketing/

Sharma, R. (2018). How Artificial Intelligence is

Changing Customer Service Forever. TechGenix. Retrieved from http://techgenix.com/ai-customer-service/

Skorupa (2019). NRF 2019: The Dawn of Experiential Shopping. RIS News. Retrieved from https://risnews.com/nrf-2019-dawn-experiential-shopping

Sowards, P. (2016). 16 Quotes that Defined AI and Intelligent Virtual Assistants in 2015. Virtually Speaking by Next It. Retrieved from http://blog.nextit.com/business/16-quotes-that-defined-ai-and-intelligent-virtual-assistants-in-2015/

TED (2017, June 6). 3 Principles for Creating Safer AI: Stuart Russell. [Video File] Retrieved from https://www.youtube.com/watch?list=PLTV3HtuyhGYFsc qmelv2M-zl_xuFRh5-s&time_continue=939&v=EBK-a94IFHY

The Ethics of Artificial Intelligence (n.d.) Integrate.ai. Retrieved from https://www.integrate.ai/ethics-of-artificial-intelligence

The Mission (2018). 9 Best Quotes about AI and Innovation. Medium.com. Retrieved from https://medium.com/the-mission/9-best-quotes-about-ai-and-innovation-8b637eb1fc82

VPUE Identity Guidelines. 9 Best Quote about AI and Innovation. Stanford. Retrieved from https://cgrado.people.stanford.edu/9-best-quotes-about-ai-and-innovation

Walker, J. (2019) Use Cases of AI for Customer Service- What's Working Now. Emerj.com. Retrieved from https://emerj.com/ai-sector-overviews/ai-for-customer-service-use-cases/

Yao, M. (2017). The Machine Intelligence Continuum. Medium. Retrieved from

https://medium.com/topbots/the-machine-intelligence-continuum-ab6aee686a2d

Printed in Great Britain
by Amazon

47855406R00078